GEDDES & GROSSET

Reference

GAELIC
PHRASEBOOK

D0452374

GEDDES & GROSSET

Reference

GAELIC
PHRASEBOOK

Martin Macdonald

Published 2007 by Geddes & Grosset,
David Dale House, New Lanark, ML11 9DJ
First published 2004, reprinted 2007

Text by Martin Macdonald

ISBN 978 1 84205 099 6

Printed and bound in Poland

POLSKABOOK

CONTENTS

5

CONTENTS

CONTENTS

HEALTH

FOR YOUR INFORMATION

THE GAELIC LANGUAGE

Failte gu Gaidhlig, canan arsaidh na h-Alba – **Welcome to Gaelic, Scotland's ancient language.**
It's also a modern one, for it is still the main language of many communities in the coastal West Highlands and especially in the islands of the Hebrides, where more than 60 per cent of the population speak it.

The Gaelic Language
Visitors to these parts cannot but be aware of the language. They hear it daily in shops and pubs and at ferry terminals, it pours from local radio stations and television programmes, road signs are bi-lingual, and for their evening's entertainment there is a wealth of Gaelic music and song on tap. From the moment they enter the Highlands they are gently enticed into the Gaelic world. Most of the place names on their road maps are Gaelic, however heavily disguised they may be with a veneer of anglicised orthography. Every topographical feature, every loch and ben, has a Gaelic name. Indeed *loch* is pure Gaelic taken into English while ben is the Gaelic *beinn* (mountain) in English dress.

Scottish Gaelic is one of the Celtic group of Indo-European languages and is closely akin to Irish. Indeed, it

11

originally came from Ireland to Argyll around the sixth century AD. The two languages still share some 75 per cent of their vocabulary in common and, with a little effort, are mutually understandable. Welsh and Breton are more distant cousins in the same group.

Gaelic expanded to cover much of Scotland by the 14th century, with the exceptions of the Borders, the eastern seaboard, and Caithness and the Northern Isles which remained under Norse influence. For a time it was the language of kings at the Scottish court. But for most of the past four centuries its boundaries were largely those of the Highlands, roughly a line sweeping eastwards from Dumbarton, through Perthshire and northeastwards to Balmoral in Aberdeenshire. To non-Gaels, ably abetted by the over-romantic pen of novelist Sir Walter Scott, it became the language of warring clans, turbulent chiefs and thieving cattle-rievers. Reality would have added a leavening of farmers, seamen, scholars, musicians and poets.

History has not been kind to the Gaels or their language. The aftermath of the Jacobite campaign and the Battle of Culloden in 1746 led to the disintegration of their traditional society. Economic hardship and enforced emigration in the 19th century meant that at one time perhaps a third of all Gaelic-speakers were to be found in Canada, where the language is still spoken. A repressive education system, which effectively banned Gaelic in schools, taught successive generations to dismiss their native language as a barrier to progress.

But these days have long gone, and in the face of adversity

Gaelic has proved remarkably resilient. Over the past 30 years its fortunes have undergone a transformation. It is not merely taught in schools but used as the medium of education in many of them, not only in its native areas but in the major Scottish cities. It is increasingly heard on radio and television and seen on public display on signs and notices. Its numbers may have decreased over generations of repression – from an estimated peak of around 250,000 to around 65,000 – but where it was once whispered in private it is now spoken openly and confidently. Never short of poets and singers and musicians, a young generation re-interprets the old songs and writes new ones for a new century. A language with ancient roots, certainly, but also a vibrant, living one.

Even a passing knowledge of Gaelic opens doors to a very distinctive culture, its history and the way of life of its people. And the willingness to try a phrase or two brings an even more welcoming smile from a people who in any case regard hospitality to the stranger as one of the major virtues. For eyes schooled on English spelling Gaelic orthography can present a daunting prospect. But once you realise that these strange *bh, mh* and *-aidh* combinations sound simply like the English v (the first two) or the English final -y (the last one), your tongue soon begins to relax round them.

Ur beatha dhan duthaich – Welcome to our country.

Key to Pronunciation

While the English alphabet has 26 letters, Gaelic uses only 18 (it has no j, k, q, v, w, x, y, z, and the h is used only to alter the quality of the preceding consonant). But by using these letters in various combinations it produces a greater variety of sounds than standard English. After the Gaelic form the phrasebook provides an elementary phonetic guide to pronunciation, based on English usage. The key to the guide is as follows:-

a	short as in "fat"
ai	short as in "bait"
aa	long as in "far"
ay	long as in "may"
e	short as in "met"
ee	short as in "meet"
i	short as in "bit"
ie	short as in "line"
o	short as in "hot"
oh	short as in "hope"
aw	long as in "dawn"
oe	long as in "more"
ow	as in "down"
u	short as in "put"
uh	short as in "grunt"
oo	long as in "poor"
ew	long as in "fewer"
y	initially or within word – as in "yield": as final syllable – as in "carry"

Gaelic has a number of sounds for which there is no direct match in standard English. Amongst the most frequently used of these are:-

ch	as in Scottish "loch"
gh	the guttural g sound in the exclamation "Ugh!"
ao	stretch the short i sound in "bin" to thrice its normal length

Although Gaelic also has a wide variety of consonant sounds, consonants in the phonetic guide (apart from the above-named combinations) should be pronounced according to standard English usage. In words throughout the guide hyphens are used to separate syllables but in speech these syllables should be run together. In fact colloquial Gaelic, like most languages, tends to run words together in continuous phrases. Syllables requiring emphasis are indicated in **bold** letters.

GETTING STARTED

Yes and no

Yes
Tha
Haa

No
Chan eil
*Chan **ail***

Gaelic has no single words for **yes** and **no**. There are at least six forms for each of them depending on the verbal form of the question.

Tha and **chan eil** are really positive and negative responses to present tense questions beginning **is/are** and really mean **is/are** and **is/are not**.

Bha and **cha robh** are the positive and negative responses to past tense questions beginning **was/were**, and **bidh** and **cha bhi** are the responses to future tense questions beginning **will**.

Another verbal form of question, **an e** (**is it . . .**), has responses **se** and **chan e**.

Everyday words and phrases

Tha and **chan eil** will be understood as **yes** and **no** even if grammatically wrong.

You

Like French, Gaelic preserves the **tu** and **vous** type of distinction between formal and informal uses of **you**. In Gaelic, **thu** is used for children and familiar friends. **Sibh** is used for older people and strangers. Although this book is written in an informal register for the most part, when meeting people for the first time **sibh** is appropriate, and so it is used here. However, **thu** can be substituted for **sibh** without grammatical offence at any time since, unlike French, the verb stays the same irrespective of person.

Everyday words and phrases

Please
Le'r toil
Lair tol

Yes, please
Tha, le'r toil
Haa, lair tol

Thank you
Tapadh leibh
Tap-uh leev

17

Being understood

Excuse me
Mo leisgeul
Moh laish-gal

No, thank you
Chan eil, tapadh leibh
Chan ail, tap-uh leev

Good
Math
Ma

OK
Ceart
Cyarst

I am very sorry
Tha mi gle dhuilich
Haa mee glay ghil-ich

Being understood

I do not speak Gaelic
Chan eil Gaidhlig agam
Chan ail Gaal-ik ak-am

I do not understand
Chan eil mi tuigsinn
Chan ail mee tik-shin

Greetings and exchanges

Can you find someone who speaks English?
Faigh sibh cuideigin le Beurla?
*Fie sheev cuj-ai-gin lai **Bayr**-luh?*

Can you help me, please?
An cuidich sibh mi, le'r toil?
*Uhn **cuj**-ich sheev mee, lair tol?*

It does not matter
Chan eil e gu difeir
*Chan ail e gu **jeef**-ir*

I do not mind
Is coma leam
*Iss **coh**-ma lum*

Please repeat that slowly
Can sin a ris gu mall, le'r toil
*Can sheen uh reesh gu mowl, lair **tol***

Greetings and exchanges

Hello
Hullo
Huh-**loh**

Hi
Haoi
Hie

Greetings and exchanges

Good evening
Feasgar math
*Fais-gar **ma***

Good morning
Madainn mhath
*Mat-ing **va***

Good night
Oidhche mhath
*Iech-uh **va***

Good-bye
Beannachd leibh
*Byan-achk **leev***

It is nice to meet you
Is math tachairt ruibh
*Iss ma **tach-irj** reev*

How are you?
Ciamar a tha sibh?
*Cya-mar uh **haa** sheev?*

I am very well, thank you
Tha mi gle mhath, tapadh leibh
*Haa mee glay **va**, tap-uh leev*

It is good to see you
Is math ur faicinn
Iss ma uhr fie-king

20

Greetings and exchanges

There are five of us
Tha sinn ann coignear
*Ha sheen own **coh-ik-nuhr***

This is — my son
Seo — mo mhac
*Sho — moh **vack***

— my husband
— mo dhuine
*— moh **ghin**-yuh*

— my daughter
— mo nighean
*— moh **nee-uhn***

— my wife
— mo bhean
*— moh **ven***

My name is . . .
Is m'ainm . . .
Iss men-uhm . . .

What is your name?
De ur n-ainm?
Jay uhr nen-uhm?

I am a student
Is oileanach mi
*Iss **ol-an-ach** mee*

21

Greetings and exchanges

I am on holiday
Tha mi air saor-laithean
Ha mee air saor-la-yuhn

I live in London
Tha mi fuireach an Lunnainn
Ha mee fur-ach uhn Lun-in

You are very kind
Tha sibh ro mhath
Ha sheev ro va

You're welcome!
Se ur beatha!
She uhr be-huh!

See you soon
Chi mi dh'aithghearr sibh
Chee mee ghie-yar sheev

I am from — **America**
Tha mi as — na Staitean Aonaichte
Haa mee ass – *na Staj-uhn Aon-ich-ji*

— **Australia**
— Strailia
— *Stral-ya*

— **Britain**
— Breatainn
— *Brait-ing*

22

Greetings and exchanges

I am from — **Canada**
Tha mi as — Canada
Haa mee ass — *Can-ad-a*

— **England**
— Sasainn
— *Sas-ing*

— **Ireland**
— Eirinn
— *Ayr-ing*

— **New Zealand**
— Zealand Nuadh
— *See-land **Noo-uh***

— **Scotland**
— Alba
— *Al-uh-ba*

— **South Africa**
— Afraca Deas
— *Afr-ac-a **Jaiss***

— **Wales**
— a' Chuimrigh
— *uh **Chim-ree***

23

Common questions

Common questions

Where?
Caite?
Caa-juh?

Where is . . .?
Caite bheil . . .?
Caa-juh vail . . .?

Where are . . .?
Caite bheil . . .?
Caa-juh vail . . .?

When?
Cuin?
Cun?

What?
De?
Jay?

How?
Ciamar?
Cya-mar?

How much?
De tha e cosg?
*Jay ha e **cosg**?*

Who?
Co?
Coe?

Why?
Carson?
Car-son?

Which?
Co aca?
*Coe **ach**-cuh?*

How long will it take?
De'n uine bheir e?
*Jayn **oon**-yuh vair e?*

How can I contact American Express/Diners Club
Ciamar a gheibh mi gu American Express/Diners Club
Cya-mar uh yaiv mee gu American Express/Diners Club

Common questions

What is the problem?
De an trioblaid?
*Jay uhn **treep**-lej?*

Do you know a good restaurant?
An aithne dhuibh deagh thigh-bidh?
*Uhn **an**-yuh yeev **joe** hie-**bee**?*

Do you mind if I . . .?
An cuir e curam oirbh ma . . .?
*Uhn cur e **coor**-im airiv ma . . .?*

What is wrong?
De tha cearr?
*Jay ha **cyaar**?*

What time do you close?
Cuin tha sibh a' dunadh?
*Cun ha sheev uh **doon**-uh?*

Where can I buy a postcard?
Caite an ceannaich mi cairt-puist?
*Caa-juh an cyan-ich mee carsj-**pushj**?*

Where can I buy currency?
Caite an ceannaich mi cuinneadh?
*Caa-juh uhn **cyan**-ich mee **coon**-yuh?*

Where can I buy traveller's cheques?
Caite an ceannaich mi seicean-siubhail?
*Caa-juh uhn **cyan**-ich mee shaic-uhn-**shoo**-il?*

25

Asking the time

Where can we sit down?
Caite am faigh sinn suidhe?
Caa-juh am fie sheen su-yuh?

Where is the toilet?
Caite bheil na goireasan?
Caa-juh vail na guhr-as-uhn?

Who did this?
Co rinn seo?
*Coe rien **sho**?*

Who should I see about this?
Co bu choir dhomh fhaicinn mu dheidhinn seo?
Coe bu chawr gho iech-king mu yay-in sho?

Will you come also?
An tig sibhse cuideachd?
*An jeek sheev-shuh **cuj**-achk?*

Asking the time

Scotland is on GMT (Greenwich Mean Time) in winter and advances one hour to BST (British Summer Time) in summer. Although many organisations now tend to use the 24-hour clock, colloquially most people express the time in terms of the 12-hour clock. In Gaelic, if the time is not immediately clear from the context of conversation and clarification is needed, a.m. is expressed by adding *'sa mhadainn (sa-**vat**-in)* to the time, and p.m. by adding *feasgar (**fais**-gur)*.

Asking the time

What time is it?
De'n uair a tha e?
Jayn oo-ar uh ha e?

It is	**— nine-thirty**
Tha e	— leth-uair an deidh naoi
Haa e	— *lai-uhr uhn jay nao*

— **six-fifteen**
— cairteal an deidh sia
— *cars-jal uhn jay shee-a*

— **a quarter past ten**
— cairteal an deidh deich
— *cars-jal uhn jay jaich*

— **a quarter to eleven**
— cairteal gu aonuair-deug
— *cars-jal gu aon-uhr-jee-ak*

— **after three o'clock**
— an deidh tri uairean
— *uhn jay tree oo-ar-uhn*

— **nearly five o'clock**
— faisg air coig uairean
— *fashk air coh-ik ou-ar-uhn*

Asking the time

It is — **twenty-five past ten**
Tha e — coig mionaidean fichead an deid hdeich
Haa e — *coh-ik meen-ej-in feech-uhd an jayjaich*

— **twenty-five to eleven**
— coig   mionaidean   fichead   gu   aonuair-deug
— *coh-ik meen-ej-in feech-uhd gu aon-uhr-jee-ag*

— **eleven o'clock**
— aonuair-deug
— *aon-uhr-jee-ag*

— **five past ten**
— coig mionaidean an deidh deich
— *coh-ik meen-ej-in uhn jay jaich*

— **half past ten**
— leth-uair an deidh deich
— *lai-uhr uhn jay jaich*

— **five to eleven**
— coig mionaidean gu aonuair-deug
— *coh-ik meen-ej-in gu aon-uhr-jee-ag*

— **ten o'clock**
— deich uairean
— *jaich oo-ar-uhn*

28

Asking the time

It is — **ten past ten**
Tha e — deich mionaidean an deidh deich
Haa e — *jaich meen-ej-in uhn jay jaich*

    — **twenty past ten**
    — fichead mionaid an deidh deich
    — *feech-uhd meen-ej uhn jay jaich*

    — **twenty to eleven**
    — fichead mionaid gu aonuair-deug
    — *feech-uhd meen-ej gu aon-uhr-jee-ag*

    It is — **early**
Tha e — trath
Ha e — *traa*

        — **late**
        — anmoch
        — ***ana**-moch*

        — **one o'clock**
        — uair
        — *oo-ar*

        — **midday**
        — meadhon-latha
        — *mee-an-laa*

        — **midnight**
        — meadhon-oidhche
        — *mee-an-**iech**-uh*

Asking the time

at about one o'clock
mu uair
mu oo-ar

at half past six
aig leth-uair an deidh sia
ek lai-uhr uhn jay shee-a

at half past eight exactly
air buille leth-uair an deidh ochd
*air **bul**-yuh lai-uhr an jay ochk*

in an hour's time
an ceann uair
an cyown oo-ar

in half an hour
an ceann leth-uair
*an cyown **lai**-uhr*

soon
a dh'aithghearr
*uh **ghie**-yar*

this afternoon
trath-noin
*traa-**nawn***

this evening
feasgar
***fais**-gar*

Common problems

this morning
madainn an diugh
*mat-ing an **ju***

tonight
an nochd
*uhn **nochk***

two hours ago
bho chionn da uair a thide
*voh chyun daa oo-ar uh **hee**-juh*

at night
air an oidhche
*air an **iech**-uh*

Common problems

I am late
Tha mi fadalach
*Ha mee **fad**-al-ach*

I cannot find my driving licence
Cha lorg mi mo chead-draibhidh
*Cha **lor**-ak mee moh chaid-**drie**-vy*

I have dropped a contact lens
Leig mi as lionsa
Leek mee ass len-suh

31

Common problems

I have lost — my credit cards
Chaill mi — mo chairtean creideis
*Chiel mee — moh **chars**-jan **craij**-ish*

— my key
— m'iuchar
— *myuch-ir*

— my traveller's cheques
— mo sheicean-siubhail
— *moh haich-ken-**shoo**-il*

I have no currency
Chan eil cuinneadh agam
*Chan ail **coon**-yuh ak-am*

I must see a lawyer
Feumaidh mi fear-lagh fhaicinn
*Fay-my mee fer-**lugh** iech-king*

My car has been stolen
Chaidh mo char a ghoid
*Chie moh **chaar** uh ghuhj*

My handbag has been stolen
Chaidh mo bhaga-laimh a ghoid
Chie moh vag-uh-liev uh ghuhj

My wallet has been stolen
Chaidh mo leabhar-poc a ghoid
*Chie moh lawr-**pawk** uh ghuhj*

AT THE AIRPORT

The Gaelic Highlands is served by a network of smaller airports with links to a central airport at Inverness, or south to Glasgow and Edinburgh airports. All three of these have developed some European and international links although most international destinations depend on further links southward to London's three airports.

While handling a relatively small volume of traffic because of the small population, the island airports at Stornoway, Benbecula, Tiree and Islay have long runways and can handle fairly large aircraft. They are a legacy from World War 2 when they were built as military air bases to guard the Western Approaches from the Atlantic and give allied shipping protection against enemy submarines. Smaller airfields have been built on the islands of Skye and Mull, and near Plockton and Oban on the mainland. Although they do not handle daily commercial flights, attempts are being made to develop them, and meanwhile they are available for small charter planes and private aircraft.

The airport on the island of Barra deserves a special mention (and perhaps a special visit) since it is probably the only tidal airfield in the world! The landing strip is on a vast, sandy beach known as *An Traigh Mhor (Uhn-traa-voer)*

Arrival

which simply means "The big beach". Twice a day the incoming tide covers the firm, white sand so that the daily flights that link it with Glasgow have to be timed with the tide-table as the main consideration. If you wish a unique landing experience it is worth a visit.

While this network of airports provides the Highlands and Islands with useful daily air services – a word of warning. Flights within Scotland are short in distance and duration but air travel is relatively expensive, perhaps because the volume of passenger traffic is not large. Islanders can be heard to complain that it costs them more to fly to Glasgow than to cross the Atlantic or to European destinations.

Arrival

Here is my passport
Seo mo chead-siubhail
*Sho moh chaid-**shoo**-il*

How long will this take?
De'n uine bheir seo?
Jayn oon-yuh vair sho?

I am attending a convention
Tha mi frithealadh co-labhairt
*Ha mee **free**-al-uh co-**lav**-irj*

34

Arrival

I am here on business
Tha mi seo air ghnothach
*Ha mee sho air **ghro**-ach*

I will be staying here for eight weeks
Bidh mi fuireach ochd seachdainean an seo
*Bee mee **fur**-ach ochk shech-ken-uhn uhn sho*

We are visiting friends
Tha sinn a' tadhal air cairdean
*Ha sheen uh **tuh**-al air **caar**-juhn*

How much do I have to pay?
De dh'fheumas mi paigheadh?
*Jay yay-mas mi **paa**-yuh?*

I have nothing to declare
Chan eil dad agam ri ainmeachadh
*Chan ail dat akam ree **enuhm**-ach-uh*

I have the usual allowances
Tha na nithean ceadaichte agam
*Ha na neech-uhn **kaid**-ich-juh akam*

This is for my own use
Is ann son m'fheum fhein tha seo
*Iss own son maym **hayn** ha sho*

Common problems and requests

Common problems and requests

Can I upgrade to first class?
Faod mi dhol suas dhan cheud chlas?
*Faod mee ghol soo-as ghan **chee-uhd** chlas?*

I have lost my ticket
Chaill mi mo bhileag
Chiel mee moh vee-lag

I have missed my connection
Chaill mi an ath phlean
Chiel mee uhn a flain

Please give me back my passport
Thoir dhomh mo chead-siubhail, le'r toil
*Hor gho moh chaid-**shoo**-il, lair tol*

The people who were to meet me have not arrived
Cha do nochd duine 'nam choinneamh fhathast
*Cha do nochk **dun**-yuh nam **chuhn**-yiv haasd*

Where can I find the airline representative?
Caite lorg mi riochdair an loidhne-adhair?
*Caa-juh lor-uhk mee rich-ker uhn lien-**aar**?*

Where do I get the connecting flight to Stornoway?
Caite faigh mi pleana ceangail Steornabhaigh?
Caa-juh fie mee plain-uh cya-il Shjawr-na-vie?

36

Common problems and requests

Where is — the bar?
Caite bheil — am bar?
Caa-juh vai — am baar?

— the departure lounge?
— an seomar-fagail?
*— uhn shaw-mar-**faag**-il?*

— the information desk?
— an deasg-fiosrachaidh?
*— uhn desg-**fees**-rachy*

— the transfer desk?
— an deasg-atharrachaidh?
*— uhn desg-**ahar**-achy*

— the toilet?
— na goireasan?
*— na **guhr**-as-uhn?*

Is there a bus into town?
Bheil bus ann dhan bhaile?
Vail buhs own ghan val-uh?

How long will the delay be?
De an dail a bhios ann?
*Jay uhn **daal** uh vees own?*

I was delayed at the airport
Chaidh dail orm aig a' phort-adhair
*Chie **daal** awr-uhm ek uh forst-**aar***

Luggage

My flight was late
Bha mo phleana fadalach
*Va moh flain-uh **fad**-al-ach*

I was held up at immigration
Chaidh dail orm aig cead-siubhail
*Chie daal awr-uhm ek kaid-**shoo**-il*

Luggage

Where is the baggage from flight number . . .?
Caite bheil na bagaichean o aireamh . . .?
Caa-juh vail na bag-ich-uhn oh aar-iv . . .?

I have lost my bag
Chaill mi mo bhaga
*Chiel mee moh **vak**-uh*

These bags are not mine
Cha leam-sa na bagaichean sin
Cha lum-sa na bak-ich-uhn sheen

Are there any baggage trolleys?
Bheil bara-bhaga ann?
*Vail bara-**vak**-uh own?*

Can I have help with my bags?
Faigh mi cuideachadh le mo bhagaichean?
*Fie mee **cuj**-ach-uh lai moh **vak**-ich-uhn?*

Luggage

Is there any charge?
Bheil dad ri phaigheadh?
Vail dat ree faa-yuh?

I will carry that myself
Giulainidh mi-fhein sin
Gyoo-leny mee hayn sheen

My baggage has not arrived
Cha d'rainig mo bhagaichean
Cha draan-ik moh vak-ich-uhn

Where is my bag?
Caite bheil mo bhaga?
Caa-juh vail moh vak-uh?

      It is — a large suticase
        Se — maileid mhor a th'ann
        She — maal-ej voer uh hown

        — a rucksack
        — mala-droma th'ann
        — mal-uh-drohm-uh hown

        — a small bag
        — baga beag a th'ann
        — bak-uh baik uh hown

No, do not put that on top
Na cuir sin air uachdar
Na kur sheen air oo-ach-kar

39

Luggage

Please take these bags to a taxi
Thoir na bagaichean sin gu tacsaidh, le'r toil
Hor na bak-ich-uhn sheen gu taxi, lair tol

Careful, the handle is broken
Socair, tha an lamh briste
***Soch**-kir, ha uhn laav breesh-juh*

This package is fragile
Tha a' phacaid seo lag
*Ha uh **fach**-kej sho **lak***

AT THE HOTEL

Tourism began developing in the Highlands some 200 years ago and has become a major industry over the past 50 years. This means that the area has a large variety of hotel accommodation, built at different times and in different styles, but all of it brought up to modern standards, usually with full en suite facilities. Thus in rural areas one may find an impressive 19th century building standing in its own grounds, once the home of a Victorian landlord or a "shooting lodge" for his guests during the autumn deer-stalking and salmon-fishing season. Outwardly and in their public rooms these hotels retain an aura of Victorian times but their bedroom facilities are fully modernised. Similarly in towns and villages old inns and hostelries can be found which combine the atmosphere of former times with modern comfort. And of course the construction of purpose-built hotels has been continuous down the years, most of them in or near the larger towns but some in tourist complexes like the Aviemore Centre.

Whatever their origins, most of these hotels provide a full range of basic facilities for their guests, whether for an overnight stay or a fortnight's holiday. Tariffs are usually per person and include breakfast, though other meals can be

Bed and breakfast accommodation

inclusive or paid separately. Most are licensed to sell drink. Usually they also offer special deals depending on length of stay or the time of year. Many of them have been awarded an excellence rating by a variety of bodies – motoring, development, or tourism organisations – though no standardised system exists throughout Scotland. Broadly speaking, the greater the number of stars (or other symbols) the more facilities on offer, and the higher the price. Food is generally good and a signifant number of Highland hotels have won major awards for cuisine.

A relatively recent development has been the northward spread of the "road-house" type of accommodation based on renting a room for the night rather than paying on an individual tariff. Such accommodation is usually much cheaper with tariffs comparable to the rest of Britain, and is normally found on the outskirts of towns where separate eating facilities are immediately adjacent or easily available.

Bed and breakfast accommodation

This sector, with the familiar B & B sign displayed outside private residences, has developed over the past 50 years and now provides a significant proportion of the area's tourist accommodation. Typically, guests are welcomed into the family home for an overnight (or longer) stay, given sleeping accommodation and a full breakfast before leaving in the morning. Some establishments also provide an evening meal

Reservations and enquiries

on request. Most B & Bs cater for five or six guests but some of them are almost mini-hotels, catering for a dozen or more guests and providing en suite facilities. While none offer the full range of hotel facilities – for example they are not licensed for drink though most allow guests to provide their own – they have a high standard of hospitality. They are also much cheaper, normally charging between a third and a half of hotel prices.

Many of the families who provide such accommodation are Gaelic-speaking, particularly in the Western Isles, Skye, Tiree and west coast mainland communities. They identify themselves as such and can be found through local tourist offices or by looking for accommodation where Gaelic is spoken on the internet. A number of hotels also pride themselves on having Gaelic-speaking staff.

Reservations and enquiries

I am sorry I am late
Tha mi duilich a bhith fadalach
*Ha mee **dul**-ich uh vee **fad**-al-ach*

I have a reservation
Ghleidh mi seomar
***Ghlay** mee **shaw**-mar*

I shall be staying until July 4th
Bidh mi fuireach gus an 4mh la dhen Iuchair
*Bee mee **fur**-ach gus uhn **ker**-iv laa yen **Yuch**-ir*

43

Reservations and enquiries

I want to stay for 5 nights
Tha mi son fuireach coig oidhcheannan
*Ha mee son **fur**-ach coh-ik **iech**-an-uhn*

Do you have a double room with a bath?
Bheil seomar dubailte le amar agaibh?
*Vail shaw-mar **doop**-il-juh lai amar ak-iv?*

Do you have a room with twin beds and a shower?
Bheil seomar le da leabaidh is frasair agaibh?
*Vail shaw-mar lai daa leby iss **fras**-ir ak-iv?*

Do you have a single room?
Bheil seomar singilte agaibh?
*Vail shaw-mar **sheen**-gil-juh ak-iv?*

I need — a double room with a bed for a child
Feumaidh mi — seomar dubailte le leabaidh son leanabh
*Fay-my mee — shaw-mar **doop**-il-juh lai leby son **len**-iv*

— a room with a double bed
— seomar le leabaidh dhubailte
— shaw-mar lai leby **ghoop**-il-juh

— a room with twin beds and bath
— seomar le da leabaidh is amar
— *shaw-mar le **daa** leby iss amar*

44

Reservations and enquiries

I need — a single room
Feumaidh mi — seomar singilte
*Fay-my mee — shaw-mar **sheen**-gil-juh*

— a single room with a shower or bath
— seomar singilte le frasair neo amar
*— shaw-mar **sheen**-gil-juh lai fras-ir naw amar*

How much is — full board
De chosgas — lan-aoigheachd
*Jay chosk-is — **laan**-ao-yachk*

— half-board
— leth-aoigheachd
*— **lai**-ao-yachk*

How much is it per night?
De chosgas oidhche?
*Jay chosk-is **iech**-uh?*

Does the price include room and breakfast?
Bheil an seomar is bracaist 'sa phris?
*Vail uhn shaw-mar iss **brach**-keshj sa **freesh**?*

Does the price include room and all meals?
Bheil an seomar is gach diadhad 'sa phris?
*Vail uhn shaw-mar iss gach **jee**-hat sa **freesh**?*

45

Reservations and enquiries

Does the price include room and dinner?
Bheil an seomar is dinnear 'sa phris?
*Vail uhn shaw-mar iss **jeen**-ir sa **freesh**?*

Can we have adjoining rooms?
Faigh sinn seomraichean ri taobh a cheile?
*Fie **sheen** shawm-rich-uhn ree **taov** uh chay-luh?*

Are there other children staying at the hotel?
Bheil clann eile fuireach 'san taigh-osda?
*Vail clown **ail**-uh fur-ach san tie-**awsd**-uh?*

Are there supervised activities for the children?
Bheil cleasan cloinne ann fo stiuireadh?
*Vail **clais**-uhn **cluhn**-yuh own foh **stew**-ruh?*

Can my son sleep in our room?
Faod mo mhac cadal 'nar seomar?
***Faod** moh **vachk** cad-al nar shaw-mar?*

Do you take traveller's cheques?
An gabh sibh seicean-siubhail?
*Uhn gav sheev shaic-uhn-**shoo**-il?*

Which floor is my room on?
De lar air am bheil mo sheomar?
*Jay **laar** air uh vail moh hyaw-mar?*

Do you have a fax machine?
Bheil inneal facs agaibh?
*Vail ing-al **facs** ak-iv?*

Reservations and enquiries

Do you have a laundry service?
Bheil seirbhis nighe agaibh?
*Vail **shair**-iv-ish **nee**-uh ak-iv?*

Do you have a safe for valuables?
Bheil falachan agaibh son nithean luachmhor?
*Vail **fal**-ach-an ak-iv son nee-uhn **loo-ach**-voer?*

Do you have any English newspapers?
Bheil paipearan Beurla agaibh?
*Vail **pie**-per-uhn **Bayr**-luh ak-iv*

Do you have a car park?
Bheil pairce charaichean agaibh?
*Vail paark-yuh **chaar**-ich-uhn ak-iv?*

Do you have a cot for my baby?
Bheil creitheall agaibh son mo leanabh?
*Vail **kray**-uhl ak-iv son moh **len**-iv?*

Do you have satellite TV?
Bheil telebhisean shaiteal agaibh?
*Vail tel-iv-**ish**-uhn **haj**-uhl ak-iv?*

What is the voltage here?
De bholtachd tha seo?
*Jay **vohlt**-achk ha sho?*

> **Is there — a casino?**
> Bheil — casino ann?
> *Vail — cas-**een**-oh own?*

Reservations and enquiries

Is there — a hairdryer?
Bheil — tiormadair-fuilt ann?
*Vail — jeer-mad-ir-**fulj** own?*

— a lift?
— ardaichear ann?
*— **aard**-ich-ir own?*

— a minibar?
— bar-beag ann?
*— baar-**baik** own?*

— a sauna?
— sauna ann?
*— **saw**-na own?*

— a swimming pool?
— amar-snamh ann?
*— amar-**snaav** own?*

— a telephone?
— fon ann?
*— **foen** own?*

— a television?
— telebhisean ann?
*— tel-iv-**ish**-uhn own?*

— a trouser press?
— beairt-bhriogais ann?
*— byarst-**vreek**-ish iwn?*

Reservations and enquiries

Is there a room service menu?
Bheil cairt-bidh seomair ann?
*Vail carshd-**bee** shaw-mer own?*

Is there a market in the town?
Bheil margaid 'sa bhaile?
*Vail **mara**-gej sa val-uh?*

Is there a Chinese resaurant?
Bheil taigh-bidh Sineach ann?
*Vail tie-**bee Sheen**-ach own?*

Is there an Indian restaurant?
Bheil taigh-bidh Innseanach ann?
*Vail tie-**bee Eesh**-en-ach own?*

Is this a safe area?
Bheil a' chearna seo sabhailte?
*Vail uh **chyaar**-nuh sho **saav**-il-juh?*

Where is the socket for my razor?
Caite bheil an toll son mo rasair?
*Caa-juh vail an towl son mo **raas**-ir?*

Is the voltage 220 or 110?
An e bholtachd da cheud is fichead neo ceud is deich a th'ann?
Uhn e volt-achk daa chee-ad iss feech-ad naw kee-ad is jaich uh hown?

Service

What time does the hotel close?
De'n uair a tha an taigh-osda dunadh?
*Jayn oo-ar uh han tie-**awsd** uh **doon-uh**?*

What time does the restaurant close?
De'n uair a tha an taigh-bidh a' dunadh?
*Jayn oo-ar uh han tie-**bee** uh **doon**-uh?*

When does the bar open?
Cuin a tha am bar a' fosgladh?
*Cun uh ha uhm **baar** uh **fosk**-luh?*

    What time is — breakfast?
    Cuin a tha — bracaist ann?
    *Cun uh ha — **brach**-keshj own?*

        — dinner?
        — an dinnear ann?
        *— uhn **jeen**-yir own?*

        — lunch?
        — biadh meadhon-la ann?
        *— bee-ugh mee-an-**laa** own?*

Service

Can I charge this to my room?
Faod mi seo chur air an t-seomar?
*Faod mee sho chur **air** uhn jaw-mar?*

Service

Can I dial direct from my room?
Faod mi fonadh direach bhon t-seomar?
*Faod mee **foen**-ugh **jeer**-ach vohn jaw-mar?*

Can I have a newspaper?
Faod mi paipear fhaighinn?
*Faod mee **pie**-per **ie**-ing?*

Can I have an outside line?
Faigh mi loidhne amach?
*Fie mee lien uh-**mach**?*

Can I have my wallet from the safe?
Faigh mi mo leabhar-poca as an fhalachan?
*Fie mee moh lawr-**pawk**-uh ass uhn al-ach-an?*

Can I have the bill please?
Faigh mi an cunntas, le'r toil?
*Fie mee uhn **coon**-das, lair tol?*

Can I hire a portable telephone?
Faod mi fon-giulain fhasdadh?
*Faod mee foen-**gew**-len asd-ugh?*

Can I make a telephone call from here?
Faod mi fonadh a seo?
*Faod mee **foen**-ugh a sho?*

Can I send this by courier?
Faod mi seo a chur le teachdaire?
*Faod mee sho a chur lai **jech**-ker-ugh?*

Service

Can I use my charge card?
Faod mi mo chairt-paighidh a chleachdadh?
*Faod mee moh charsj-**paa**-y uh chlech-kuh?*

Can I use my personal computer here?
Faod mi mo choimpiutair pearsanta chleachdadh an seo?
*Faod mee moh chom-**pew**-ter pers-ant-ugh chlech-kuh uhn sho?*

Can I use traveller's cheques?
Faod mi seicean-siubhail a chleachdadh?
*Faod mee shaicean-**shoo**-il uh **chlech**-kuh?*

Can we have breakfast in our room, please?
Faod sinn bracaist fhaighinn 'nar seomar, le'r toil?
*Faod sheen **brach**-keshj ie-ing nar shaw-mar, lair tol?*

Can you recommend a good local restaurant?
An urrainn dhuibh deagh thaigh-bidh ionadail a mholadh?
*Uhn ur-ing yeev joe hie-**bee** een-ad-al uh **vol**-ugh?*

I want to stay an extra night
Tha mi son fuireach oidhche bharrachd
Ha mee son fur-ach iech-uh var-achk

Do I have to change rooms?
Feum mi an seomar atharrachadh?
*Faym mee uhn shaw-mar **ahar**-ach-ugh*

I need an early morning call
Feumar mo ghairm trath
***Faym**-ar moh ghair-am traa*

52

Service

I need — a razor
Feumaidh mi — rasair
Faym-y mee — **raas**-ir

— some soap
— siabann
— **shee**-ban

— some toilet paper
— paipear-glanaidh
— pie-per-**glan**-y

— some towels
— searadairean
— **sher**-ad-er-uhn

I need to charge these batteries
Feumar na batraidhean seo bheothachadh
*Faym-ar na **bat**-ree-uhn sho **vyaw**-ach-ugh*

I want to press these clothes
Tha mi son an t-aodach seo iarnaigeadh
*Ha mee son uhn **taod**-ach sho **ee-arn**-ig-ugh*

Is there a trouser press I can use
Bheil beairt-bhriogais ann a chleachdas mi
*Vail byarst-**vreek**-ish own uh **chlech**-kas mee*

Please fill the minibar
Lionaibh am bar-beag, le'r toil
***Lee-uhn**-iv uhm baar-**baik**, lair tol*

53

Service

Please leave the bags in the lobby
Fagaibh na bagaichean anns an trannsa, le'r toil
Faag-iv na bak-ich-uhn owns uhn trown-sa, lair tol

Please send this fax for me
Cuiribh am facs seo air falbh dhomh, le'r toil
Cur-iv uhm fax sho air fal-iv gho, lair tol

Please turn the heating off
Cuiribh dhe an teas, le'r toil
Cur-iv ye uhn jais, lair tol

Please wake me at 7 o'clock in the morning
Duisgibh mi aig seachd uairean 'sa mhadainn, le'r toil
Doosh-kiv mee ek shechk oo-ar-uhn sa vat-ing, lair tol

Where can I send a fax?
Co as a chuireas mi facs?
Coe ass uh chur-is mee fax?

Can I have — my key, please?
Faigh mi — m'iuchair, le'r toil?
Fie mee — myuch-ir, lair tol?

— an ashtray?
— soitheach-luath?
— se-ach-loo-uh?

— another blanket?
— plangaid eile?
— Plang-ej ail-uh?

54

Service

Can I have — another pillow?
Faigh mi — cluasag eile?
*Fie mee — **cloo**-as-ak **ail**-uh?*

— some coat hangers?
— crochain-chota?
*— croch-en-**chaw**-tuh?*

— some notepaper?
— paipear-sgriobhaidh?
*— pie-per-**skree**-vy?*

Has my colleague arrived yet?
An d'rainig mo chompanach fhathast?
*Uhn **draan**-ik moh **chowm**-pan-ach haasd?*

I am expecting a fax
Tha duil agam ri facs
*Ha **dool** ak-am ree fax*

My room number is 22
Se dha-air-fhichead aireamh mo sheomar
*She ghaa-air-eech-ad **aar**-iv moh **hyaw**-mar*

Please can I leave a message?
Faod mi fios fhagail, le'r toil?
*Faod mee fees **aak**-el, lair tol?*

Problems

Problems

Where is the manager?
Caite bheil am manaidsear?
*Caa-juh vail uhm **mad**-ij-ir?*

I cannot close the window
Chan urrainn dhomh an uinneag a dhunadh
*Chan **ur**-ing gho uhn **un**-yak uh **ghoon**-ugh*

I cannot open the window
Chan urrainn dhomh an uinneag fhosgladh
*Chan **ur**-ing gho uhn **un**-yak osk-lugh*

The air conditioning is not working
Chan eil am beairt-aile ag obair
*Chan ail uhm byarst-**aal**-uh ak **ohb**-ir*

The room key does not work
Chan eil iuchair an t-seomair ag obair
*Chan ail **yuch**-ir uhn **jawm**-ir ak **ohb**-ir*

The bathroom is dirty
Tha an seomair-ionnlaid salach
*Ha uhn shawm-ir-**yoon**-lej sal-ach*

The heating is not working
Chan eil an teas ag obair
*Chan ail uhn **jais** ak **ohb**-ir*

56

Checking out

The lighting is not working
Chan eil an solas ag obair
Cha ail uhn sol-is ak ohb-ir

The room is not serviced
Cha deach an seomair a reiteach
Cha jech uhn shawm-ir uh ray-jach

The room is too noisy
Tha cus fuaim 'san t-seomair
Ha cus foo-im san jawm-ir

There are no towels in the room
Chan eil searadairean 'san t-seomair
Cha ail sher-ad-er-uhn san jawm-ir

There is no hot water
Chan eil uisge teth ann
Chan ail oosh-guh jai own

There is no plug in the washbasin
Chan eil plucan 'sa mhias-ionnlaid
Chan ail pluk-an sa vee-as-yoon-lej

Checking out

I have to leave tomorrow
Feumaidh mi fagail am maireach
Fay-my mee faak-el uhm maar-ach

Checking out

We will be leaving early tomorrow
Bidh sinn a' fagail trath am maireach
*Bee sheen uh **faak-el traa** uhm **maar**-ach*

Could you have my bags brought down?
An urrainn dhuibh mo bhagaichean fhaighinn anuas?
*Uhn **ur**-ing yeev moh **vak**-ich-uhn **ie**-ing uh-**noo**-as?*

Could you order me a taxi?
Faigh sibh tacsi dhomh?
*Fïe sheev **tax**-y gho?*

Thank you, we enjoyed our stay
Tapa leibh, chord an turas ruinn
***Tap**-uh leev, **chawrt** uhn **tur**-is reen*

OTHER ACCOMMODATION

Apart from hotels and B & B establishments, other accommodation options in the Highlands include self-catering cottages, farmhouse holidays, boating holidays, camping and hostelling. Again local tourist offices or holiday brochures can advise on what is available, but increasingly the internet is a useful tool in this respect, either by looking for a particular category of accommodation or choosing a particular locality where all local options are usually identified.

Self-catering

Traditional farm cottages and croft houses adapted to tourist needs are widely available throughout the Highlands. There is also some purpose-built accommodation, usually in the form of wooden chalets of Scandinavian design. And in recent years larger complexes of self-catering units have been built, frequently attached to nearby hotels and leisure centres, often in woodland or waterside settings which allow access to outdoor activities.

Most accommodation will provide basic cooking facilities

Boating holidays

and utensils with an adequate range of cutlery and crockery. In some cases, however, you may be asked to provide your own bed linen and towels. Such requirements should be clarified when booking, as also should the methods of paying for lighting and heating.

Holiday cottages are normally rented by the week for an all-in sum which will vary according to the time of year. The relative cheapness or otherwise of your holiday will therefore depend on the number of people in the party shairng the facilities. Late cancellations might mean a cottage is available for a shorter period at the last minute.

Boating holidays

Cabin cruisers are available for hire on the Caledonian Canal, which stretches the length of the Great Glen from Inverness on the north-east coast to Fort William at the head of Loch Linnhe on the west coast. Most of the length of the canal is taken up by three freshwater lochs – Loch Lochy, Loch Oich and Loch Ness, world-famed for its legendary "Monster". The cruisers vary in size and accommodation (and thus in price) and are equipped with the basic domestic facilities of a holiday cottage, with the added advantage of offering a mobile holiday through some of the most spectacular scenery in Scotland. Cruisers are normally hired for weekly periods but at slack times shorter last-minute hires might be available.

Sea-going holiday cruises are available from a number of

Camping

west coast ports, particularly Oban. The ships involved are normally small yachts or small coastal steamers or fishing boats converted to take passengers. They might carry between half-a-dozen and a dozen paying guests who, if they wish, can also learn to take part in crewing the ship. Such cruises along the west coast and out to the islands can vary in duration from a week to ten days or a fortnight. Prices vary depending on each individual cruise.

Camping

Given the popularity of the Highlands as an area for outdoor activities – particularly hiking, hill-walking and climbing – it is no surprise that it should be well provided with camp sites where tents can be erected for an overnight stay, or longer, for a daily fee. Popular mountain areas – such as Torridon, Glencoe, the Skye Cuillins and the Cairngorms – boast a number of them based at strategic distances around their peripheries. They can also be found at most east coast seaside resorts such as Nairn or Dornoch. Only in the Western Isles, where sudden gales sweeping in from the Atlantic can make camping a precarious business, are they in short supply.

Most camp sites provide basic washing facilities such as showers, toilets and laundry provision. Some of them may have a small shop stocked with a limited range of general goods. Many of them are within easy range of eating facilities, perhaps an adjacent hotel restaurant or a nearby village.

Camping rough

But in the more remote ones dedicated to the climbing fraternity you may have to depend on what food and cooking facilities you bring with you. Few if any of them have standing tents or equipment for hire.

Camping rough

With the proliferation of camping sites (and campers) the former sight of a lonely tent in the heather in some remote glen is scarce nowadays. But some cross-country hikers still prefer isolation. Most roads in the west Highlands are unfenced and normally no-one objects to seeing a lone tent on the open hill, though you may find yourself face to face with an irate gamekeeper if you disturb his quarry during the autumn deer-stalking season. Remember also that these open moorlands carry livestock so take your rubbish with you. Discarded cans and bottles can injure cattle and sheep.

Never camp on enclosed agricultural land without the specific permission of the farmer or crofter to whom it belongs. In fact, it's better to seek local advice about camping on open ground as well. And a final word of advice. Whether on a camp site or open ground take an adequate supply of insect repellent with you. Tiny it might be, but there is nothing that can nip quite as ferociously as a Highland midge (meanbh-chuileag – **men**-*iv*-*chul*-*ack)* on a moist and muggy autumn day.

Taking a caravan

Many of the larger camp sites, particularly in the central Highlands and on the east coast, cater also for caravans. In fact some of them have a number of residential caravans permanently on site. They are generally equipped on much the same lines as holiday cottages and rented out on much the same basis. In the islands and on the west coast some crofters have two or three such caravans for rent.

Taking your own caravan to the Highlands involves the same considerations as towing a caravan in the rest of Britain, though perhaps to a greater degree. Of the main arterial routes into the Highlands only the A9 is dual carriageway, and that for only brief sections of its length once you are north of Perth; most of it is a two-lane highway. Restricted to 50mph that means frequent stops to release the inevitable build-up of traffic behind. Most of the west coast highways, and the scenic coastal routes, still have sections of single-track road with lay-bys and passing-places. That means even more frequent stops, both to allow oncoming vehicles to pass and to relieve the traffic build-up behind. The island ferries carry caravans, but given that fares are based on the length of vehicles, crossing with car and caravan can be relatively costly.

The Scottish Youth Hostels Association (SYHA) has been established for over 70 years and now runs over 60 hostels

Renting a house

throughout the country. They are to be found in cities, villages and remote and isolated rural glens. They range from historic buildings and castles to modern purpose-built accommodation and renovated shepherds' cottages. They aim to provide relatively cheap overnight accommodation, frequently in small dormitories, where guests can have the use of cooking facilities. The organisation has wide international links with similar bodies, and arranges package holidays based on outdoor, environmental and cultural activities.

In recent years a number of privately-owned hostels have emerged offering similarly cheap accommodation, along much the same lines of providing dormitory beds and basic cooking facilities. They tend to be found in towns and villages and usually describe themselves as "backpackers' " or "students' " hostels.

Renting a house

We have rented this villa
Tha sinn air an taigh seo ghabhail
*Ha sheen air an **tie** sho **ghav**-el*

Here is our booking form
Seo a' bhileag gleidhidh againn
*Sho uh vee-lak **glay**-y **ak**-in*

We need two sets of keys
Feumaidh sinn da ghad iuchraichean
***Fay**-my sheen daa ghad **yuch**-rich-uhn*

Renting a house

Can I contact you on this number?
Faigh mi air an aireamh seo sibh?
*Fie mee air uhn **aar-iv** sho sheev?*

Where is the bathroom?
Caite bheil an seomair-ionnlaid?
*Caa-juh vail uhn shawm-ir-**yoon**-lej?*

How does this work?
Ciamar a tha seo ag obair?
*Cya-mar uh ha sho ak **ohb**-ir?*

I cannot open the shutters
Chan urrainn dhomh na comhlaichean fhosgladh
*Chan **ur**-ing gho na **cawl**-ich-uhn **osk**-lugh*

Can you send a repairman?
An lorg sibh fear-caraidh?
*Uhn lor-ak sheev fer-**caar**-y?*

Is the water heater working?
Bheil inneal-teas an uisge ag obair?
*Vail een-yal-**jais** uhn **oosh**-guh ak **ohb**-ir?*

Is the water safe to drink?
Bheil e sabhailte an t-uisge ol?
*Vail e **saav**-il-juh uhn **toosh**-guh awl?*

Is there any spare bedding?
Bheil aodach-leapa a bharrachd ann?
*Vail aod-ach-**lep** uh **var**-achk own?*

65

Renting a house

The cooker does not work
Chan eil an cucair ag obair
*Chan ail uhn **cuk**-er ak **ohb**-ir*

The refrigerator does not work
Chan eil am frids ag obair
*Chan ail uhm **frij** ak **ohb**-ir*

The toilet is blocked
Tha na goireasan tachdte
*Ha na **guhr**-as-an **tach**-juh*

There is a leak
Tha ao-dion ann
*Ha **ao**-jen own*

We do not have any water
Chan eil uisge againn
*Chan ail **oosh**-guh ak-in*

When does the cleaner come?
Cuin a thig an neach-glanaidh?
*Cun uh heek uhn nyech-**glan**-y?*

Where is the fuse box?
Caite bheil am bocsa-dealain?
*Caa-juh vail uhm boc-suh-**jal**-en?*

Where is the key for this door?
Caite bheil iuchair an dorais seo?
*Caa-juh vail **yuch**-ir uhn **dor**-ish sho?*

Around the house

bath
amar
am-ar

bathroom
seomair-ionnlaid
shawm-ir-yoon-lej

bed
leabaidh
leb-y

brush
sguabach
skoo-ab-ach

can opener
fosglair-chana
fosk-ler-chan-uh

chair
cathair
ca-hir

cooker
cucair
cuk-er

corkscrew
sgriubh-arca
screw-aark-uh

cup
cupa
cup-uh

fork
forca
fork-uh

glass
glainne
glan-yuh

inventory
cunntas
coon-das

kitchen
cidsin
keej-in

knife
sgian
skee-uhn

Around the house

mirror
sgathan
skaa-han

spoon
spainn
spaa-ing

pan
pana
pan-uh

stove
stobha
staw-vuh

plate
truinnsear
treen-sher

table
bord
bawrd

refrigerator
frids
freej

tap
srup
strewp

rubbish
smodal
smod-al

toilet
taigh-beag
tie-baik

sheet
anart
an-uhrd

vacuum cleaner
glanadair-deoghail
glan-ad-er-jaw-il

sink
since
seen-kuh

washbasin
mias-ionnlaid
mee-as-yoon-lej

Useful camping questions

Can we camp in your field?
Faod sinn campachadh anns a' bhuaile agaibh?
*Faod sheen **cowm-pach-ugh** owns uh **voo-il** ak-iv?*

Can we camp near here?
Faod sinn campachadh faisg air seo?
*Faod sheen **cowm-pach-ugh** fashk air sho?*

Please can we pitch our tent here?
Faod sinn ar teanta chur an seo, le'r toil?
*Faod sheen ar **tent**-uh chur uhn sho, lair tol?*

Can we park our caravan here?
Faod sinn ar carabhan a pharcadh an seo?
*Faod sheen ar car-uh-**van** uh **fark**-uh uhn sho?*

Do I pay in advance?
Am paigh mi ro-laimh?
*Uhm **paa**-y mee ro-**liev**?*

Do I pay when I leave?
Am paigh mi nuair dh'fhagas mi?
*Uhm **paa**-y mee nar **ghaak**-is mee?*

Useful camping questions

Is there a more sheltered site?
Bheil larach nas fhasgaich ann?
*Vail **laar**-ach nas **ask**-ich own?*

Is there a restaurant or a shop on the site?
Bheil taigh-bidh neo buth air an larach?
*Vail tie-**bee** naw **boo** air uhn **laar**-ach?*

Is there another camp site near here?
Bheil larach campa eile faisg air seo?
*Vail **laar**-ach **cowm**-puh **ail**-uh **fashk** air sho?*

Is this the drinking water?
An e seo an t-uisge son ol?
*Uhn e sho uhn **toosh**-guh son **awl**?*

The site is very wet and muddy
Tha an larach lan uisge is eabar
*Ha uhn **laar**-ach **laan** oosh-guh iss aib-ar*

Where are the toilets?
Caite bheil na goireasan?
*Caa-juh vail na **guhr**-as-uhn?*

Where can I buy gas?
Caite an ceannaich mi gas?
*Caa-juh uhn **cyan**-ich mee gas?*

Where can I have a shower?
Caite faigh mi frasair?
*Caa-juh fie mee **fras**-er?*

Around the camp site

Where can we wash our dishes?
Caite an nigh sinn ar soithichean?
*Caa-juh uhn **nee** sheen ar **se-ich-uhn?***

Around the camp site

air mattress
babhstair gaoithe
*bow-ster **gee**-huh*

backpack
poca-droma
*pohk-uh-**drohm**-uh*

bucket
bucaid
***buk**-ej*

camp bed
leabaidh pasgaidh
*leb-y **pask**-y*

camp chair
cathair pasgaidh
*ca-hir **pask**-y*

can opener
fosglair-chana
*fosk-ler-**chan**-uh*

cup
cupa
***cup**-uh*

fire
teine
***jain**-uh*

flashlight
lasair
***las**-er*

fly sheet
brat dunaidh
*brat **doon**-y*

folding table
bord pasgaidh
*bawrd **pask**-y*

fork
forca
***fork**-uh*

71

Around the camp site

frying pan
aghann
ugh-uhn

penknife
sgian-bheag
skee-uhn-vaik

ground sheet
brat-lair
brat-laar

plate
truinnsear
treen-sher

ground
talamh
tal-iv

rucksack
mala-droma
maal-uh-drohm-uh

guy line
stagh
stuh

shelter
fasgadh
fask-ugh

knife
sgian
skee-uhn

tent pole
crann teanta
crown tent-uh

mallet
fairche
far-chyuh

tent
teanta
tent-uh

matches
maidsichean
maj-ich-uhn

thermos flask
searrag-theth
shar-ag-hai

pail
peile
pail-uh

torch
leus
lee-as

72

Hostelling

sleeping bag
poca cadail
pohk-uh cad-il

spoon
spainn
spaa-ing

stove
stobha
staw-vuh

tent peg
cipean
keep-an

Hostelling

Is there a youth hostel near here?
Bheil ostail oigridh faisg air seo?
Vail osd-el awk-ry fashk air sho?

Can we stay here five nights?
Faod sinn fuireach an seo coig oidhcheannan?
Faod sheen fur-ach uhn sho coe-ik iech-an-uhn?

Can we stay until Sunday?
Faod sinn fuireach gu Di-domhnaich?
Faod sheen fur-ach gu Jee-dawn-ich?

Hostelling

Here is my membership card
Seo mo chairt-ballrachd
*Sho moh charsj-**bowl**-rachk*

I do not have my card
Chan eil mo chairt agam
*Chan ail moh **charsj** ak-am*

Can I join here?
Faod mi gabhail ann an seo?
*Faod mee **gav-el own** uhn sho?*

Are you open during the day?
Bheil sibh fosgailte feadh an la?
*Vail sheev **fosk-il-juh** fyugh uhn **laa**?*

Can I use the kitchen?
Faod mi an cidsin a chleachdadh?
*Faod mee uhn **keej-in** uh **chlech**-kuh?*

What time do you close?
De an uair a tha sibh a' dunadh?
*Jayn oo-ar uh ha sheev uh **doon**-ugh?*

Do you serve meals?
Bheil sibh a' tabhainn biadh?
*Vail sheev uh **taf**-ing **bee**-uh?*

> **— to take away?**
> — son a thoirt air falbh?
> *— son uh horst air **fal**-iv?*

Childcare

Can you warm this milk for me?
An teasaich sibh am bainne seo dhomh?
*Uhn **jais**-ich sheev uhm **ban**-yuh sho gho?*

Do you have a high chair?
Bheil cathair ard agaibh?
*Vail **ca**-hir **ard** ak-iv?*

Is there a baby-sitter?
Bheil suil-leanaibh ann?
*Vail sool-**len**-iv own?*

Is there a cot for our baby?
Bheil creitheall ann dhan leanabh?
*Vail **crai**-hil own ghan **len**-iv?*

Is their a paddling pool?
Bheil amar plubraich ann?
*Vail am-ar **plub**-rich own?*

Is there a swimming pool?
Bheil amar snamh ann?
*Vail am-ar **snaav** own?*

Is there a swing park?
Bheil pairce chleas ann?
*Vail paark-yuh **chlais** own?*

Childcare

I am very sorry. That was very naughty of him
Tha mi uamhasach duilich. Bha siod gle mhi-mhodhail
*Ha mee **oo-a-**vas-ach dul-ich. Va shud **glay vee-**voh-ghal*

It will not happen again
Cha tachair e ris
*Cha **tach-**ir e **ree-**ish*

How old is you daughter?
De an aois a tha ur nighean?
*Jayn aosh uh ha uhr **nee-**uhn?*

My daughter is 7 years old
Tha mo nighean seachd bliadhna dh'aois
*Ha moh **nee-**uhn shechk **bleen-**uh ghaosh*

My son is 10 years old.
Tha mo mhac deich bliadhna dh'aois
*Ha moh vak jaich **bleen-**uh ghaosh*

She goes to bed at nine o'clock
Tha I dol a laighe aig naoi uairean
*Ha ee dol ugh **le-**uh ek nao oo-ar-uhn*

We will be back in two hours
Bidh sinn air ais an da uair a thide
*Bee sheen air ash uhn **daa** oo-ar uh **heej-**uh*

Where can I buy some disposable nappies
Caite an ceannaich mi badain caitheimh?
*Caa-juh uhn **cyan-**ich mee bad-en **cie-**hiv?*

Childcare

Where can I change the baby?
Caite an atharraich mi na badain?
*Caa-juh uhn **a**-har-ich mee na bad-en?*

Where can I feed my baby?
Caite am biadh mi an leanabh?
*Caa-juh uhm **bee**-uh mee uhn **len**-iv?*

GETTING AROUND

Transport

Apart from air services, the Highlands' other public transport links with the rest of Scotland and Britain are provided
by regular train services to Glasgow and Edinburgh and
south to London *(see page 93)*, and by more frequent coach
services to these same destinations *(see page 92)*. In general
terms travelling by rail is more expensive than travelling by
road.

Internally also the area has a network of rail and coach services linking its far-flung villages and rural communities
with main centres like Inverness and Fort William. These
services tend to be less frequent than the southern ones
simply because most residents in the area own cars, and tend
to use them even for long journeys because of the greater
flexibility of travel they offer.

The islands off the west coast are linked to the mainland
by regular car-ferry services *(see page 100)*.

Asking for directions

Where is — the art gallery?
Caite bheil — taigh nan ealain?
*Caa-juh vail — **tie** nan **yal**-en?*

— the post office?
— oifis a' phuist?
*— of-ish uh **fusht**?*

— the Tourist Information Service?
— Fiosrachadh Turasachd?
*— **Fees**-rach-ugh **Tur**-as-achk?*

Can you tell me the way to the bus station?
An stiuir sibh mi gu steisean nam busaichean?
*Uhn shtewr sheev mee gu **stay**-shin nam **buhs**-ich-uhn?*

I am lost
Tha mi air chall
*Ha mee air **chowl***

I am lost. How do I get to the Royal Hotel?
Tha mi air chall. Ciamar a gheibh mi dhan Taigh-osda
Rioghail?
*Ha mee air **chowl**. Cya-mar uh yaiv mee ghan Tie-**awsd**-uh
Ree-ghal?*

Asking for directions

Can you show me on the map?
An seall sibh dhomh air a' mhap?
*Uhn **showl** sheev gho air uh **vap**?*

May I borrow your map?
Faigh mi iasad dhen mhap?
*Fie mee **ee-as**-ad yen **vap**?*

We are looking for a restaurant
Tha sinn a' lorg taigh-bidh
*Ha sheen uh **lor-ak** tie-**bee***

Where are the toilets?
Caite bheil na goireasan?
*Caa-juh vail na **guhr**-as-uhn*

I am looking for the Tourist Information Office
Tha mi a' lorg Oifis an Turasachd
*Ha mee uh **lor**-ak Of-ish uhn **Tur**-as-achk*

I am trying to get to the market
Tha mi a' fiachainn ris a' mhargaid fhaighinn
*Ha mee uh **fee**-ach-in reesh uh **var**-ag-ej ie-ing*

Can you walk there?
An gabh e coiseachd?
*Uhn gav e **cosh-achk**?*

Is it far?
Bheil e fada?
*Vail e **fad**-uh?*

Directions – by road

I want to go to the theatre
Tha mi son dhol dhan taigh-cluiche
*Ha mee son ghol ghan tie-**cleech**-uh*

Is there a bus that goes there?
Bheil bus a' dol ann?
*Vail **buhs** uh dol own?*

Where do I get a bus for the city centre?
Caite faigh mi bus son meadhon a' bhaile?
*Caa-juh fie mee buhs son **mee-an** uh **val**-uh?*

Is there a train that goes there?
Bheil treana a' dol ann?
*Vail **tren** uh dol own?*

Directions – by road

Where does this road go to?
Caite bheil an rathad seo a' dol?
*Caa-juh vail uhn **raad** sho dol?*

Do I turn here for Inverness?
An tionndaidh mi an seo son Inbhirnis?
*Uhn **joon**-die mee uhn sho son Een-ir-**neesh**?*

How do I get onto the motorway?
Ciamar a gheibh mi dhan phriomh-rathad?
*Cya-mar uh **yaiv** mee ghan **freev**-raad?*

81

Directions – by road

How far is it to Glasgow?
De an t-astar a th'ann gu Glaschu?
*Jayn **tasd**-ir uh hown gu **Glas**-cho?*

How long will it take to get there?
De an uine bheir e faighinn ann?
*Jayn **oon**-yuh vair e **fie**-ing own?*

I am looking for the next exit
Tha mi a' lorg an ath fhosgladh
*Ha mee uh **lor**-ak an a **osk**-lugh*

Is there a filling station near here?
Bheil steisean connaidh faisg air seo?
*Vail stay-shin **cohn**-y fashk air sho?*

Is this the right way to the supermarket?
An e seo an slighe ceart dhan mhor-mhargadh?
*Uhn e sho uhn **shlee**-uh **cyarst** ghan vohr-**var**-ag-ej?*

Which is the best route to Oban?
De an slighe as fhearr dhan Oban?
*Jayn **shlee**-uh as **yar** ghan **Awb**-an?*

Which is the fastest route?
De an slighe as luaithe?
*Jayn **shlee**-uh as **loo**-a-yuh?*

Which road do I take to Portree?
De an rathad a bheir a Phortruigh mi?
*Jayn raad uh vair uh Forst-**ree** mee*

Directions – what you may hear

Directions – what you may hear

Theirig — cho fada ri . . .
Hair-ik — cho fad-uh ree..
Go — as far as . . .

— dhan laimh chli
— ghan liev chlee
— to the left

— dhan laimh dheas
— ghan liev yais
— to the right

Theirig a dh'ionnsaigh . . .
Hair-ik uh yoon-sy . . .
Go towards . . .

Tha e — aig crois an rathaid
Ha e — ek crosh uh raw-ij
It is — at the crossroads

— mun cuairt an oisein
— muhn coo-arst uhn osh-en
— around the corner

— fo'n drochaid
— foen droch-ij
— under the bridge

83

Directions – what you may hear

Tha e — an deidh nan solas
Ha e — uhn jay nan sol-as
It is — after the traffic lights

— ri taobh an taigh-dhealbh
— ree taov uhn tie-yal-iv
— next to the cinema

— air an ath lar
— air uhn a laar
— on the next floor

— mu choinneamh steisean an reile
— mu chuhn-yiv stay-shin uhn rayl-uh
— opposite the railway station

— thall an sin
— howl uh sheen
— over there

Theirig tarsaing na sraide
Hair-ik tars-ing na straaj-uh
Cross the street

Lean na soighnichean son — an ath chrois rathaid
Len na sien-ich-uhn son — uhn a chrosh-raw-ij
Follow the signs for — the next junction

— a' phriomh-rathaid
— uh freev-raw-ij
— the motorway

Directions – what you may hear

Lean na soighnichean son na cearnaig
*Len na **sien**-ich-uhn son na **cyaar**-nek*
Follow the signs for the square

Lean direach romhad
*Len **jeer**-ach **ro**-ad*
Keep going straight ahead

Gabh an lamh chli
*Gav uhn lav **chlee***
Turn left

Gabh an lamh dheas
*Gav uhn lav **yais***
Turn right

Feumaidh sibh tilleadh
*Fay-my sheev **jeel**-ugh*
You have to go back

Gabh a' cheud rathad air an laimh dheas
*Gav uh **chee-ad** raad air uhn liev **yais***
Take the first road on the right

Gabh rathad Ghearrloch
*Gav raad **yaar**-loch*
Take the road for Gairloch

Gabh an darna rathad air an laimh chli
*Gav uhn **daar**-nuh raad air uhn liev **chlee***
Take the second road on the left

Hiring a car

Hiring a car

Most of the large international car hire firms operate throughout Scotland, including the Highlands. They can be found at all major airports and in most large cities and towns, offering a wide range of cars at differing prices. Many of them allow their customers to pick up a car at one point and drop it off at another at the end of the hire, thus giving greater flexibility for a travelling holiday. In the islands and towns on the west coast mainland cars can usually be hired from local firms and garages.

A driving licence from any major country is usually sufficient to be allowed to hire, as long as it can be read in English as well as the original language. Most hire firms insist that the driver be over 25 years of age, though some firms will accept drivers over 23. Insurance is normally included in the hire price. It is often worth arranging car hire in advance through an international firm or a fly-drive deal.

I want to hire a car
Tha mi son car fhasdadh
*Ha mee son **caar asd**-ugh*

I need it for 2 weeks
Feumaidh mi e son cola-deug
*Fay-my mee e son coh-la-**jee**-ak*

Hiring a car

Can I hire a car?
Faod mi car fhasdadh?
*Faod mee **caar asd**-ugh?*

Can I hire a car with an automatic gearbox?
Faod mi car fein-ghidhreach fhasdadh?
*Faod mee **caar** fayn-yeer-ach **asd**-ugh?*

Please explain the documents
Minichibh na bileagan, le'r toil
***Meen**-ich-iv na **beel**-ak-uhn, lair tol*

We will both be driving
Bidh an dithis againn a' draibheadh
*Bee uhn **jeesh** ak-in uh **driev**-ugh*

> **Do you have — a large car?**
> Bheil — car mor agaibh?
> *Vai — **caar moer** ak-iv?*

>> **— a smaller car?**
>> — car nas lugha agaibh?
>> *— **caar** nas **lao**-uh ak-iv?*

>> **— an automatic?**
>> — fein-ghidhreach agaibh?
>> *— fayn-**yeer**-ach ak-iv?*

>> **— an estate car?**
>> — car oighreachd agaibh?
>> *— **caar ier**-achk ak-iv?*

Hiring a car

I want to leave the car at the airport
Tha mi son an car fhagail aig a' phort-adhair
*Ha mee son an **caar aak**-el ek uh forst-**aar***

I would like to leave the car at the airport
Bu mhath leam an car fhagail aig a' phort-adhair
*Bu **va** lum an **caar aak**-el ek uh forst-**aar***

Is there a charge per mile?
Bheil cosgais ann gach mile?
*Vail **cos**-kish own gach **meel**-uh?*

Must I retun the car here?
Feum mi an car a thilleadh an seo?
***Faym** mee an **caar** uh **heel**-yugh uhn sho?*

Can I pay for insurance?
Faod mi paigheadh son arachas?
*Faod mee **paa**-yugh son **aar**-ach-as?*

Do I have to pay a deposit?
Feum mi tasgadh a phaigheadh?
***Faym** mee **task**-ugh uh **faa**-yugh?*

How does the steering lock work?
Ciamar a tha a' ghlas-stiuiridh ag obair?
*Cya-mar uh ha uh ghlas-**shtew**-ry ak **ohb**ir?*

I would like a spare set of keys
Bu mhath leam gad iuchraichean a bharrachd
*Bu **va** lum gat **yuch**-rich-uhn uh **var**-achk*

By taxi

Where is reverse gear?
Caite bheil an gidhear deiridh?
*Caa-juh vail uhn **geer jai**-ry?*

Where is the tool kit?
Caite bheil na h-innealan?
*Caa-juh vail na **heen**-al-uhn?*

Please show me how to operate the lights
Seall dhomh mar tha na solais ag obair, le'r toil
***Showl** gho mar ha na **sol**-ish ak **ohb**-ir, lair tol*

Please show me how to operate the windscreen wipers
Seall dhomh mar tha na suathairean ag obair, le'r toil
***Showl** gho mar ha na **soo-a-**her-uhn ak **ohb**-ir, lair tol*

By taxi

Taxis are easily available in most parts of the Highlands. They can be identified by a local authority licensing plate on the back and a roof sign which carries their telephone number. In the larger towns they normally park at specified taxi ranks and fares are metered. Most taxis are limited to four passengers – though there are larger ones – and it is normal to offer the driver a tip.

Taxis can also be hired for a half-day or a day for a scenic tour or a visit to places of special tourist interest. In such cases a fee should be negotiated before setting off.

By taxi

Where can I get a taxi
Caite faigh mi tacsaidh
*Caa-juh fie mee **tax**-y*

Take me to the airport, please
Thoir dhan phort-adhair mi, le'r toil
***Hor** ghan forst-**aar** mee, lair tol*

The bus station, please
Steisean nam busaichean, le'r toil
*Stay-shan nam **buhs**-ich-uhn, lair tol*

Please show us around the town
Seall dhuinn am baile, le'r toil
***Showl** yeen uhm **bal**-uh, lair tol*

Please take me to this address
Thoir dhan t-seoladh seo mi, le'r toil
***Hor** ghan **jawl**-ugh sho mee, lair tol*

Could you put the bags in the boot, please?
An cuir sibh na bagaichean 'sa chul, le'r toil?
*Uhn cur sheev na **bak**-ich-uhn sa **chool**, lair tol*

Turn left, please
An lamh chli, le'r toil
*Uhn lav **chlee**, lair tol*

Turn right, please
An lamh dheas, le'r toil
*Uhn lav **yais**, lair tol*

By taxi

Wait for me, please
Fan rium, le'r toil
Fan rum, lair tol

Can you come back in one hour?
An till sibh an uair a thide?
Uhn jeel sheev uhn oo-ar uh heej-uh?

Please wait here for a few minutes
Fan an seo son mionaid neo dha, le'r toil
Fan uhn sho son meen-ej naw ghaa, lair tol

Please, stop at the corner
Stad aig an oisean, le'r toil
Stad ek uhn osh-uhn, lair tol

Please, wait here
Fan an seo, le'r toil
Fan uhn sho, lair tol

I am in a hurry
Tha cabhag orm
Ha caf-ag or-am

Please hurry, I am late
Dean cabhag, le'r toil, tha mi fadalach
Jen caf-ag, lair tol, ha mee fad-al-ach

How much is it per mile?
De tha e cosg 'sa mhile?
Jay tha e cosk sa veel-uh?

91

By bus

How much is that, please?
De tha sin, le'r toil?
*Jay ha **sheen,** lair tol?*

Keep the change
Cum an iomlaid
***Coom** uhn **yum**-lej*

By bus

Most large towns in the Highlands have frequent and regular local bus services, and most outlying rural areas are linked to major centres like Inverness, Fort William and Oban by daily services. They make frequent stops at villages en route and the longer distance ones may run only once or twice daily each way. Trunk routes south to cities like Glasgow and Edinburgh have fast and frequent services daily, most of which do not stop en route.

Does this bus go to the castle?
Bheil am bus seo a' dol dhan chaisteal?
*Vail uhm **buhs** sho uh dol ghan **chash**-jal?*

How frequent is the service?
De cho tric's a tha e ruith?
*Jay cho **treek** suh ha e **ree**?*

What is the fare to the city centre?
De am faradh gu meadhon a' bhaile?
*Jay uhm **far**-ugh gu **mee**-an uh **val**-uh?*

By train

Where should I change?
Caite am bu choir dhomh atharrachadh?
*Caa-juh uhm bu **chawr** gho a-har-ach-ugh?*

Which bus do I take for the football stadium?
De am bus a ghabhas mi gu pairc a' bhall-coise?
*Jay uhm **buhs** uh **ghav**-as mee gu **paark** uh val-**cosh**-uh?*

Where do I get the bus for the airport?
Caite faigh mi bus a' phuirt-adhair?
*Caa-juh fie mee **buhs** uh furst-**aar**?*

Will you tell me when to get off the bus?
An innis sibh dhomh cuin a dh'fhagas mi am bus?
*Uhn **eensh** sheev gho cun uh **ghaak**-as mee uhm **buhs**?*

When is the last bus?
Cuin a tha am bus mu dheireadh ann?
*Cun uh ha uhm **buhs** mu **yair**-ugh own?*

By train

The three main rail routes from the south into the Highlands run from Glasgow (and Edinburgh) north to Inverness via Perth and the central Highlands; from Glasgow west to Oban; and from Glasgow north to Fort William via the west Highlands. A fourth line runs west to Inverness from Aberdeen on the east coast of Scotland.

From Inverness a line runs north to Wick, and another westwards to Kyle of Lochalsh on the west coast. And from

By train

Fort William a line runs to Mallaig on the west coast, some 40 miles south of Kyle of Lochalsh. These latter two vie with any in Europe for scenic beauty. They skirt spectacular mountains, meander along quiet inland lochs, and finally open onto magnificent vistas of sea-lochs and islands. Day return trips to either Kyle of Lochalsh or Mallaig are worthwhile for the scenery alone.

For rail enthusiasts steam trains run on the Fort William-Mallaig line during the tourist season, and on a now disused branch line between Aviemore and Boat of Garten in the central Highlands.

Timetables and fares for all rail services can be found on the internet and at mainline stations and tourist offices.

Can I buy a return ticket?
Faod mi bileag tillidh a cheannach?
*Faod mee bee-lag jeel-y uh **chyan**-ach?*

A return to Aberdeen, please
Bileag tillidh gu Abaireadhain, le'r toil
*Bee-lag **jeel**-y gu Ab-ir-e-**e**-ing, lair tol*

A return to Edinburgh, first class
Bileag tillidh gu Dun-eideann, a' cheud chlas
*Bee-lag **jeel**-y gu Doon-**ay**-jin, uh **chee**-ad chlas*

A single ticket to Glasgow, please
Bileag shingilte gu Glaschu, le'r toil
*Bee-lag **heen**-gil-juh gu **Glas**-chu, lair tol*

94

By train

Can I book a seat?
Faod mi suidheachan a ghleidheadh?
*Faod mee **suy-ach-an** uh **ghlay-ugh**?*

Is the train full?
Bheil an treana lan?
*Vail uhn **tren-uh** **laan**?*

Second class. A window seat, please
An darna clas. Suidheachan uinneig, le'r toil
*Uhn **daar-nuh** clas. **Suy-ach-an un-ek**, lair tol*

Can I take my bicycle?
Faod mi mo rothair thoirt leam?
*Faod mee moh **ro-hir horst** lum*

Is this the train for London?
An e seo treana Lunnainn?
*Uhn e sho **tren-uh Lun-in**?*

What are the times for the trains to Perth?
De na h-amannan son treanaichean Pheairt?
*Jay na **ham-an-uhn** son **tren-ich-uhn Fyarst**?*

How long do I have before my next train leaves?
De an uine th'agam mus fag an ath threana?
*Jayn **oon-yuh** hak-am mus **faak** uhn a **hren-uh**?*

Where can I buy a ticket?
Caite an ceannaich mi bileag?
*Caa-juh uhn **cyan-ich** mee **bee-**lag?*

By train

Where do I have to change?
Caite feum mi atharrachadh?
*Caa-juh faym mee **a**-har-ach-ugh?*

Where do I pick up my bags?
Caite an tog mi mo bhagaichean?
*Caa-juh uhn **tohk** mee moh **vak**-ich-uhn?*

Can I check in my bags?
Faod mi mo bhagaichean a chur a-staigh?
*Faod mee moh **vak**-ich-uhn uh chur uh-**stie**?*

I want to leave these bags in the left-luggage
Tha mi son na bagaichean seo fhagail 'san stor-bhaga
*Ha mee son na **bak**-ich-uhn sho **aak**-el san stawr-**vak**-uh*

How much is it per bag?
De tha e cosg gach baga?
*Jay ha e **cosk** gach **bak**-uh?*

I shall pick them up this evening
Togaidh mi iad feasgar
***Tohk**-y mee ad **fais**-gar*

I want to book a seat on the sleeper to London
Tha mi son suidheachan a ghleidheadh air an treana-chadail gu Lunnainn
*Tha mee son **suy**-ach-an uh **ghlay**-ugh air uhn tren-uh-**chad**-il gu **Lun**-in*

By train

Is there — a left-luggage office
Bheil — stor-bhaga ann
*Vail — stawr-**vak**-uh own*

— food available on the train?
— biadh ri fhaighinn air an treana?
*— **bee**-ugh ree **ie**-ing air uhn **tren**-uh?*

— a buffet car?
— bufaidh ann?
*— **buf**-y own?*

— a dining car?
— car bidh ann?
*— caar-**bee** own?*

Where is the departure board?
Caite bheil an clar fagail?
*Caa-juh vail uhn claar **faak**-el?*

What time does the train leave?
Cuin a tha an treana a' fagail?
*Cun uh ha uhn **tren**-uh uh **faak**-el?*

Do I have time to go shopping?
Bheil uine agam dhol dha na buithnean?
*Vail **oon**-yuh ak-am ghol gha na **boon**-yuhn?*

What time is the last train?
Cuin a tha an treana mu dheireadh ann?
*Cun uh ha uhn **tren**-uh mu **yair**-ugh own?*

97

By train

When is the next train to Stirling?
Cuin a tha an ath threana gu Sruighle?
*Cun uh ha uhn a **hren**-uh gu **Stree-lie**?*

When is the next train to Kyle of Lochalsh?
Cuin a tha an ath threana gu Caol Loch-aillse?
*Cuin uh ha uhn a **hren**-uh gu Caol Loch-**iesh**?*

Which platform do I go to?
De an cidhe dhan teid mi?
*Jay uhn **kee**-uh ghan **jayj** mee?*

Is this a through train?
An e treana dhireach a tha seo?
*Uhn e **tren-ih** yeer-ach ha sho?*

Is this the Oban train?
An e seo treana an Obain?
*Uhn e sho **tren-uh** uhn **Awb-en**?*

Do we stop at Tyndrum?
An stad sinn aig Taigh-an-droma?
*Uhn **stad** sheen ek Tie-uhn-**drohm**-uh?*

What time do we get to Kingussie?
Cuin a ruigeas sinn Ceann-ghiuthsaich?
*Cun uh **reek**-as sheen Cyan-**yews**-ich?*

Are we at Blair Atholl yet?
Bheil sinn am Blar Athall fhathast?
Vail sheen uhm Blar A-hal haasd?

98

By train

Are we on time?
Bheil sinn ri uair?
Vail sheen ree oo-ar?

Can you help me with my bags?
An cuidich sibh mi le mo bhagaichean?
Uhn cuj-ich sheev mee lai moh vak-ich-uhn?

Is this seat taken?
Bheil an suidheachan seo air a ghabhail?
Vail uhn suy-ach-an sho air uh ghav-el?

May I open the window?
Faod mi an uinneag fhosgladh?
Faod mee uhn un-yak osk-lugh?

My wife has my ticket
Tha mo bhileag aig mo bhean
Ha moh vee-lag ek moh ven

I have lost my ticket
Chaill mi mo bhileag
Chiel mee moh vee-lag

Smoking is forbidden on the train
Chan eil smocadh ceadaichte air an treana
Chan ail smok-ugh caid-ich-juh air uhn tren-uh

This is my seat
Seo mo shuidheachan-sa
Sho moh huy-ach-an-suh

By car ferry

Where is the toilet?
Caite bheil an taigh-beag?
Caa-juh vail uhn tie-baik?

Why have we stopped?
Carson a tha sinn air stad?
Car-son uh ha sheen air stad?

By car ferry

All the islands off the west coast are served by fast, modern car ferries from mainland ports. In the north, the crossing from Ullapool to Stornoway in Lewis takes less than three hours. From Uig in Skye a ferry runs on a tri-angular route to Tarbert in Harris and Lochmaddy in North Uist, each leg of the voyage taking less than two hours. (Skye itself is served by a bridge at Kyle of Lochalsh, and two short ferry crossings from Glenelg and Mallaig on the mainland).

Farther south, a number of ferries sail from the mainland port of Oban to the islands of Mull, Lismore, Colonsay, Coll, Tiree, Barra and South Uist. The shortest and most frequent crossing is to Mull, which takes 40 minutes, while the long haul to Barra and South Uist normally takes six and a half hours. From mainland Kintyre ferries also sail to the islands of Islay and Gigha, and a number of small ferries sail on short inter-island crossings while other small islands are linked by a system of causeways and bridges. In all, some 22 of the west coast islands are served by car ferry.

By car ferry

The inter-linking ferry system allows travellers to cross to the islands by one service, drive through a number of islands using inter-island ferries, and then return to the mainland by another crossing. There are concessionary rates for such tours, variously known as "Island Hopscotch" or "Island Rover" tickets, which make them cheaper to use than standard return journeys by the same crossing.

Ferry timetables and tariffs can be found at tourist offices, shipping company offices, and on the internet. Since ferries can be extremely busy at the height of the tourist season all bookings should be made well beforehand. Tickets are normally bought at pierhead offices before boarding the vessel, and vehicles should have checked in at the pierhead at least half-an-hour before departure times.

How do I get to the pier?
Ciamar a gheibh mi dhan chidhe?
*Cya-mar uh yaiv mee ghan **chee**-uh?*

We have to be there an hour before the ferry leaves
Feumaidh sinn a bhith ann uair a thide mus fag an aiseag
*Fay-my sheen uh vee own **oo-ar** uh **heej**-uh mus **faak** uhn **ash**-ak*

What does it cost to take a car across?
De tha e cosg car a thoirt anull?
*Jay ha e **cosk caar** uh horj uh-**nool**?*

101

By car ferry

Does that include the driver?
Bheil sin a' gabhail a-staigh an draibhear?
*Vail sheen uh **gav**-el uh-**stie** uhn **drie**-ver?*

How long does the crossing to Barra take?
De an uine a bheir a' bhoidse Bharraidh?
*Jay uhn **oon**-yuh vair uh **vawj**-uh **Var**-ie?*

Does the same boat go to Tiree?
An e an aon bhata tha dol gu Tiriodh?
*Uhn e uhn aon **vaat**-uh ha dol gu **Jir**-ugh?*

What port does the Islay ferry leave from?
De am port as am bheil aiseag Ile a' falbh?
*Jay uhm **porst** ass uhm vail **ash**-ak **Eel**-uh fal-iv?*

I have a booking for the Mull ferry
Tha aite gleidhte agam air aiseag Mhuile
*Ha **aaj**-uh **glay**-juh ak-am air **ash**-ak **Vul**-uh*

I see three boats at the pier. Which one goes to Mull?
Chi mi tri bataichean aig a' chidhe. Co an te tha dol a Mhuile?
*Chyee mee **tree baat**-ich-uhn ek uh **chee**-uh. **Coh** uhn jay ha dol uh **Vul**-uh?*

When do we have to go on board?
Cuin a dh'fheumas sinn dhol air bord?
***Cun** uh **yaym**-is sheen ghol air **bawrsd**?*

102

By car ferry

Do I have to drive the car on board?
Feum mi fhein an car a chur air bord?
*Faym mee **hayn** uhn **caar** uh chur air **bawrsd**?*

There are three of us. The driver and two others
Tha triuir againn ann. An draibhear agus dithis eile
*Ha **trewr** ak-in own. Uhn **drie**-ver agh-is **jeesh** ail-uh*

Do we return by the same route or is there another way?
An till sinn air an aon t-slighe neo bheil doigh eile ann?
*Uhn **jeel** sheen air uhn aon **dlee**-uh naw vail dawy **ail**-uh own?*

How many vehicles can that ferry carry?
Cia-meud carbad a bheir an aiseag ud leatha?
*Cya-**mee**-ad **car**-ab-ad uh vair uhn **ash**-ak uhd **le**-uh?*

Can we get food on board?
Faigh sinn biadh air bord?
*Fie sheen **bee**-ugh air **bawrsd**?*

Is there a bar on board?
Bheil bar air bord?
*Vail **baar** air **bawrsd**?*

Can we get ferries between the islands without returning to the mainland?
Faigh sinn aiseagan eadar na h-eileanan gun tilleadh gu tir-mor?
*Fie sheen **ash**-ak-uhn **aid**-uhr na **hail**-an-uhn guhn **jeel**-ugh gu jeer-**moer**?*

103

By car ferry

Can we get one ticket to take us round the islands?
Faigh sinn aon bhileag a bheir timcheall nan eilean sinn?
*Fie sheen **aon veel**-ak uh vair jeem-ich-al nan ail-an sheen?*

What time will we arrive at Barra?
De an uair aig an ruig sinn Barraidh?
*Jayn **oo-ar** ek uhn rik sheen **Bar**-ie?*

Will it be dark at that time?
Am bi e dorcha nuairsin?
Uhm bee e dor-ach-uh noo-ar-shin?

How good are the island roads?
De cho math's a tha rathaidean an eilein?
*Jay cho **mas** uh ha **rawj**-uhn uhn ail-en?*

Is there plenty of accommodation there?
Bheil gu leoir aitichean fuirich ann?
*Vail gu **lawr** aaj-ich-uhn **fur**-ich own?*

Can we get petrol on the island?
Faigh sinn peatrol air an eilean?
*Fie sheen **pet**-rol air uhn **ail**-uhn?*

Is there a garage if we break down?
Bheil garaids ann ma bhristeas sinn sios?
*Vail **gar**-ej own ma vreesh-jis sheen **shee**-is?*

What is the weather likely to be?
De an coltas a th'air an t-side?
*Jayn **cohl**-as uh hair uhn jee-juh?*

By car ferry

Are there likely to be strong winds?
Bheil gaoth laidir dualach a bhith ann?
*Vail gao **laaj-ir doo-al-ach** uh vee own?*

Could it be stormy out at sea?
Faodadh e bhith garbh aig muir?
***Faod-ugh** e vee **gar-iv** ek **mur**?*

Does the boat toss a lot in wild weather?
Am bi am bata tulgadh cus ri droch shide?
*Uhm bee uhm **baat-uh tul-ak-ugh cus** ree droch **heejuh**?*

Does the weather delay sailings often?
Am bi an side tric a' cur maille air seoladh?
*Uhm bee uhn **sheej-uh treek** uh cur **mal-yuh** air **shawl-ugh**?*

What happens if we are trapped on the island?
De thachras ma theid ar glacadh air an eilean?
*Jay hach-ris ma **haij** ar **glak-ugh** air uhn **ail-uhn**?*

Where can we get anti-seasickness pills?
Caite faigh sinn bilichean son tinneas-mara?
*Caa-juh fie sheen **beel-ich-uhn** son **jeen-yas mar-uh**?*

The officer is waving us to go aboard
Tha an t-oifigear 'gar smeideadh air bord
*Ha uhn **dof-ik-er** gar **smay-juh** air **bawrsd**

105

DRIVING

Driving in the Highlands is subject to exactly the same laws, regulations and speed limits as in the rest of Britain. There are no motorways in the area. Most of the main routes are two-lane highways though short sections of the A9 – the main arterial route northwards – are dual carriageway. At busy times of year there can be considerable tailbacks of fairly slow-moving traffic so the motorist must be constantly on guard against the temptation to overtake in dangerous circumstances.

Towards the west coast and in the islands, where many of the most scenically rewarding routes are to be found, many of the secondary roads – and indeed short sections of some main roads – are still single-track. They can be narrow and hilly – indeed mountainous – with unexpected sharp bends and they demand special care. Such roads have frequent laybys and passing-places where motorists should stop to allow oncoming traffic to pass. But these passing-places are also intended to let slow-moving traffic allow faster traffic piling up behind to pass. Tourists meandering along enjoying the scenery should also have a constant eye in the rearview mirror. That impatient motorist immediately behind may be the local doctor bent on urgent business.

Vast stretches of Highland roads are unfenced and thus

Traffic and weather conditions

open to livestock and wild animals. Sheep frequently graze on roadside verges and are prone to jump across the path of an oncoming vehicle without warning. In crofting and farming districts cattle are frequently driven along the road and motorists should give them priority. At certain times of year deer also graze near roads. Night driving needs special care since deer and cattle are notoriously difficult to pick up in car headlights in the dark, and hitting them can cause immense damage to a vehicle and its occupants.

In some areas of the northern Highlands a motorist can travel many miles without finding a wayside filling station. It is thus a wise precaution to fill up with fuel at one of the larger towns before setting out on the trip. This also makes economic sense since fuel tends to become more expensive the farther one is from a main centre. In an area like the Highlands memberships of one of the main motoring organisations can be a useful investment, especially for someone who does not know the area well.

Traffic and weather conditions

Are there any hold-ups?
Bheil dail sam bith ann?
*Vail **daal** sam bee own?*

Is the traffic heavy?
Bheil na rathaidean trang?
*Vail na **rawj-uhn** trang?*

Traffic and weather conditions

Is the traffic one-way?
An e aon taobh a tha e dol?
*Uhn e aon **taov** uh ha e dol?*

Is there a different way to the stadium?
Bheil rathad eile dhan phairce?
*Vail **raad ail**-uh ghan **faark**?*

Is there a toll on this highway?
Bheil cis air an rathad-mhor seo?
*Vail **keesh** air uhn **raad-voer** sho?*

What is causing this traffic jam?
De's aobhar dhan tachdadh seo?
*Jays **aov-uhr** ghan **tach-kugh** sho?*

What is the speed limit?
De an t-astar ceadaichte?
*Jayn **tast-uhr kaid-ich-juh**?*

What time does the car park close?
Cuin a tha a' phairce-charaichean a' dunadh?
***Cun** uh ha uh **faar-kyuh-chaar-ich-uhn** uh **doon-ugh**?*

What time is the rush hour?
Cuin a tha an uair thrang?
***Cun** uh ha uhn **oo-ar hrang**?*

Do I need snow chains?
Feum mi seinichean sneachda?
*Faym mee **shayn-ich-uhn shnech-kuh**?*

108

Parking

Is the pass open?
Bheil am bealach fosgailte?
Vail uhm byal-ach fosk-il-juh?

Is the road to Drumochter snowed up?
Bheil rathad Dhruim-uachdar duinte le sneachda?
Vail raad Ghrim-oo-ach-kir doon-juh lai shnech-kuh?

When will the road be clear?
Cuin a bhios an rathad fosgailte?
Cun uh vees uhn raad fosk-il-juh?

Parking

In most town centres parking is available in designated car parks on the pay-and-display system where parking for a certain length of time is paid for at a meter and the ticket is displayed on the car windscreen. Some towns have limited on-street parking under the same system. In small villages and rural areas parking is free at the discretion of the motorist – as long, of course, as the car is not a hazard to other motorists or blocks an access. Laybys and passing places on single-track roads should not be used for parking, especially overnight, since that would hinder the flow of traffic. Most hotels and B & B establishments have their own parking.

Is it safe to park here?
Bheil e sabhailte parcadh an seo?
Vail e saav-il-juh park-ugh uhn sho?

Parking

Can I park here?
Faod mi parcadh an seo?
*Faod mee **park**-ugh uhn sho?*

Do I need a parking ticket?
Feum mi bileag parcaidh?
*Faym mee bee-lak **park**-y?*

Where do I pay?
Caite am paigh mi?
*Caa-juh uhm **paay** mee?*

Where is there a car park?
Caite bheil pairce-charaichean?
*Caa-juh vail **paark**-yuh **chaar**-ich-uhn?*

How long can I stay here?
De'n uine dh'fhaodas mi fuireach an seo?
*Jayn **oon**-yuh **ghaod**-is mee **fur**-ach uhn sho?*

> **Do I need — coins for the meter?**
> Feum mi — buinn son a' mhiodair?
> *Faym mee — **buyn** son uh **veet**-er?*

> > **— parking lights?**
> > — solais parcaidh?
> > *— **sol**-ish **park**-y?*

At the service station

In some remote and sparsely populated districts service stations may be few and far between, so it is wise to fill up at main centres and re-fill whenever there is an opportunity. Fuel in the Highlands tends to be dearer than the rest of Britain, and the farther one is from main centres the dearer it becomes. All service stations supply Unleaded Petrol and most have Diesel. LPG (Liquid Petroleum Gas) is available at some stations but by no means all.

In some areas which have a strong tradition of Sabbath observance, notably the islands of Lewis and Harris and some communities on the north-west mainland, most service stations may be closed on Sunday, so it is a wise precaution to fill up on Saturday evening.

Do you take credit cards?
An gabh sibh cairtean creideas?
*Uhn gav sheev **cars-juhn craij-ish?***

Can you clean the windscreen?
An glan sibh an uinneag aghaidh?
*Uhn **glan** sheev uhn **un**-yak **ugh**-y?*

Fill the tank please
Lion an tanca, le'r toil
***Lee**-uhn uhn **tank**-uh, lair tol*

111

At the service station

25 litres of — unleaded petrol
Coig air fhichead liotair de — pheatrol gun luaidh
Coh-ik air eech-ad leet-er de — fet-rol gun loo-y

— 2 star
— dha rionnag
— ghaa run-ak

— 4 star
— cheithir rionnag
— chai-hir run-ak

— diesel
— dhiesel
— ghee-sil

I need some distilled water
Feumaidh mi uisge-tarraingte
Fay-my mee ush-kyuh tar-ing-juh

Check the tyre pressure, please
Fiach cruas nan taidhrichean, le'r toil
Fee-ach croo-as nan tie-rich-uhn, lair tol

The pressure should be 2.3 at the front and 2.5 at the rear
Bu choir dhan chruas a bhith dha puing tri air an toiseach
is dha puing coig air a' chul
*Bu chawr ghan chroo-as uh vee ghaa pu-ing tree air uhn
tosh-ach iss ghaa pu-ing coh-ik air uh chool*

112

Breakdowns and repairs

Check — the oil
Fiach — an t-ola
Fee-ach — uhn tol-uh

— the water
— an t-uisge
— *uhn tush-kyuh*

Breakdowns and repairs

Most local garages in the Highlands can deal with roadside breakdowns, but since a breakdown can happen in an isolated spot where the nearest garage is miles away and difficult to contact it is worth being a member of the Automobile Association or the Royal Automobile Club. Given that roadside telephone facilities may also be distant a mobile phone could also be useful. Baisic breakdown aids such as tow ropes, jump leads and torches are also worth carrying.

Can you give me — a push?
An urrainn dhuibh — mo phutadh?
Uhn ur-ing yeev — moh fut-ugh

— a tow?
— mo tharraing?
— *moh har-ing*

Can you send a recovery truck?
An urrainn dhuibh carbad togail a chur thugam?
Uhn ur-ing yeev car-ab-ad tohk-el uh chur huk-am?

113

Breakdowns and repairs

Can you take me to the nearest garage?
An urrainn dhuibh mo thoirt dhan gharaids as fhaisge?
*Uhn **ur**-ing yeev moh **horsj** ghan **ghar**-ej ass **ash**-kyuh?*

Is there a telephone nearby?
Bheil fon faisg oirnn?
*Vail **fon** fashk awrn?*

Can you find out what the trouble is?
An lorg sibh an trioblaid?
*Uhn **lor**-ak sheev uhn **treep**-lej?*

Can you give me a can of petrol, please?
An toir sibh dhomh canastair peatroil, le'r toil?
*Uhn dor sheev gho **can**-is-der **pet**-rol, lair tol?*

Can you repair a flat tyre?
An urrainn dhuibh taidhir iseal a charadh?
*Uhn **ur**-ing yeev **tier eesh**-al uh **chaar**-ugh?*

Can you repair it for the time being?
An urrainn dhuibh a charadh son greiseag?
*Uhn **ur**-ing yeev uh **chaar**-ugh son **graish**-ak?*

Can you replace the windscreen wiper blades?
An urrainn dhuibh lannan ura chur anns na suathairean?
*Uhn **ur**-ing yeev **lan**-uhn **oor**-uh **chur** owns na **soo-a**-har-en?*

My car has broken down
Tha mo char air bristeadh sios
*Ha moh **chaar** air **breesh**-jugh **shee**-as*

114

Breakdowns and repairs

My car will not start
Cha thoisich an car agam
*Cha **haw**-shich uhn **caar** ak-am*

Do you have an emergency fan belt?
Bheil crios gaotharain eiginn agaibh?
*Vail crees **gao-har-en ayk**-in ak-iv?*

Do you have jump leads?
Bheil cabaill leum agaibh?
*Vail caab-il **laym** ak-iv?*

Do you have the spare parts?
Bheil na pairtean ura agaibh?
*Vail na **paars**-juhn oor-uh ak-iv?*

I have a flat tyre
Tha taidhir iseal agam
*Ha **tier eesh-al** ak-am*

I have blown a fuse
Tha fius air leaghadh
*Ha **fews** air **lyuh**-ugh*

I have locked myself out of the car
Tha mi air an car a ghlasadh orm fhein
*Ha mee air uhn **caar** uh **ghlas**-ugh or-am **hayn***

I have locked the ignition key inside the car
Tha mi air an iuchair-adhnaidh a ghlasadh 'sa char
*Ha mee air uhn **yuch**-ir-**aon**-y uh **ghlas**-ugh sa **chaar***

Breakdowns and repairs

I have run out of petrol
Ruith mi amach a peatrol
*Ree mee uh-**mach** a **petrol***

I need a new fan belt
Feumaidh mi crios gaotharain ur
*Fay-my mee crees-**gao-har-en** **oor***

I think there is a bad connection
Cha chreid mi nach eil droch cheangal ann
*Cha chraij mee nach ail droch **chyaa-uhl** own*

Is there a mechanic here?
Bheil meicnic an seo?
*Vail **maichk**-in-ik uhn sho?*

The engine has broken down
Tha an t-einnsean air bristeadh
*Ha uhn **tain**-shin air **breeshjuh***

There is something wrong
Tha rud-eigin cearr
*Ha **rud-ek-in** **cyaar***

There is something wrong with the car
Tha rud-eigin cearr air a' char
*Ha **rud-ek-in** **cyaar** air uh **chaar***

Will it take long to repair it?
An toir e fada 'ga charadh?
*Uhn dor e **fat-**uh ga **chaarugh?***

116

Breakdowns and repairs

Is it serious?
Bheil e cudtromach?
*Vail e **cud**-rom-ach?*

My windscreen has cracked
Sgain an uinneag aghaidh
***Skaan** uhn **un**-yak **ugh**-y*

The air-conditioning does not work
Chan eil am beairt-aile ag obair
*Chan ail uhm byarsd-**aal**-uh ak **ohb**-ir*

The battery is flat
Tha am batraidh sios
*Ha uhm **bat**-ry **shee**-is*

The engine is overheating
Tha an t-einnsean a' fas ro theth
*Ha uhn **tain**-shin uh **faas** ro **hai***

The exhaust pipe has fallen off
Tha a' phiob thraoghaidh air tuiteam dhe
*Ha uh feeb-**hrao**-y air **tut**-yim ye*

There is a leak in the radiator
Tha an reideatair ag ao-dion
*Ha uhn **rayj**-at-er ak **aoj**-en*

117

Accidents and the police

Accidents and the police

In the case of minor bumps and scrapes, where no injury or major damage has been involved, it is not necessary to call the police. It is sufficient for the parties concerned to exchange names and addresses and details of their respective insurance companies. If an accident does involve injury the police, and perhaps other emergency services like ambulance and fire brigade, should be called. If the local police number is not available they can be contacted by dialling 999 or 112.

There has been an accident
Tha tubaist air a bhith ann.
*Ha **tub-esj** air uh vee own*

We must call an ambulance
Feumaidh sinn carbad-eiridinn a ghairm
*Fay-my sheen **car**-ab-ad-**air**-ij-in uh **yair**-am*

We must call the police
Feumaidh sinn am polas a ghairm
*Fay-my sheen uhm **pol**-is uh **yair**-am*

What is your name and address?
De ur n-ainm is ur seoladh?
*Jay uhr **nen**-am iss uhr **shaw**-lugh?*

118

Accidents and the police

You must not move
Chan fhaod sibh gluasad
*Chan **aod** sheev **gloo**-as-ad*

Do you want my passport?
Bheil sibh ag iarraidh mo chead-siubhail?
*Vail sheev ak **yeer**-y moh chyaid-**shoo**-il?*

He did not stop
Cha do stad e
*Cha do **stad** e*

He is a witness
Se fianais a th'ann
*She **fee-uhn-ish** uh hown*

He overtook on a bend
Ghabh e seachad air lub
*Ghav e **shech**-ad air **loob***

He ran into the back of my car
Ruith e a-staigh an cul mo char
*Ree e uh-**stie** uhn **cool** moh **chaar***

He stopped suddenly
Stad e gu h-obann
*Stad e gu **hop-uhn***

He was moving too fast
Bha e siubhal ro luath
*Va e **shoo**-il ro **loo-uh***

119

Accidents and the police

Here are my insurance documents
Seo mo phaipearan arachais
Sho moh fie-per-uhn aar-ach-ish

Here is my driving licence
Seo mo chead draibhidh
Sho moh chaid drie-vy

I could not stop in time
Cha b'urrainn dhomh stad an am
Cha bur-ing gho stad uhn owm

I did not see the bicycle
Chan fhaca mi an rothair
Chan achk-uh mee uhn ro-hir

I did not see the sign
Chan fhaca mi an soighne
Chan achk-uh mee uhn sie-nuh

I did not understand the sign
Cha do thuig mi an soighne
Cha do hik mee uhn sie-nuh

I am very sorry. I am a visitor
Tha mi uamhasach duilich. Se coigreach a th'annam
Ha mee oo-av-as-ach dul-ich. She coykrach uh hun-am

I did not know the speed limit
Cha b'aithne dhomh an t-astar ceadaichte
Cha ban-yuh gho uhn tast-ar cyaid-ich-juh

Accidents and the police

How much is the fine?
De'n cain a th'ann?
*Jayn **caa**-ing uh hown?*

I have not got enough money. Can I pay at the police station?
Chan eil airgiod gu leoir agam. Faod mi paigheadh aig steisean nam polas?
*Chan ail **er**-ik-ad gu **lawr** ak-am. Faod mee **paa**-yugh ek stay-shin nam **pol**-is?*

I have not had anything to drink
Cha robh dad agam ri ol.
*Cha ro **dat** ak-am ree **awl***

I was only driving at 30mph
Cha robh mi dol ach deich mile fichead 'san uair
*Cha ro mee dol ach **jaich meel**-uh **feech**-ad san **oo-ar***

I was overtaking
Bha mi dol seachad
*Va nee dol **shech**-ad*

I was parking
Bha mi parcadh
*Va mee **park**-ugh*

My car has been towed away
Chaidh mo char a tharraing air falbh
*Chie moh **chaar** uh **har**-ing air fal-iv*

121

Accidents and the police

That car was too close
Bha an car ud ro fhaisg
*Va uhn **caar** uhd ro **ashk***

The brakes failed
Dh'fhairtlich am breic
Ghar-lich** uhm **brechk

The car number was . . .
B'e aireamh a' chair . . .
*Be **aar-iv** uh **chaar** . . .*

The car skidded
Shleamhnaich an car
Lown-ich** uhn **caar

The car swerved
Thug an car siaradh
*Huk uhn **caar** shee-ar-ugh*

The car turned right without signalling
Ghabh an car gu deas gun rabhadh
*Ghav uhn **caar** gu **jais** gun **rav**-ugh*

The road was icy
Bha deigh air an rathad
*Va **jie** air uhn **raad***

The tyre burst
Spreadh an taidhir.
***Spruh** uhn **tie**-ir*

122

Car parts

accelerator
brogaire
brok-er-uh

aerial
aer-ghath
er-gha

air filter
siolan aile
shee-lan aal-uh

alternator
aldarnadair
alt-er-naad-er

antifreeze
ana-reothaidh
an-uh-raw-y

axle
aiseal
ash-al

battery
batraidh
bat-ry

bonnet
bonaid
bon-ej

boot
ciste
keesh-juh

brake fluid
ola bhreic
ola vrek

brakes
breicean
brek-uhn

bulb
balgan
bal-ak-an

bumper
bragadair
brak-ad-er

car phone
fon cair
foen caar

Car parts

carburettor
carbradair
caar-brad-er

dynamo
dineamo
jeen-uh-moh

child seat
suidheachan leanaibh
suy-ach-an len-iv

electrical system
seol dealain
shawl jal-en

choke
tachdair
tach-ker

engine
einnsean
ien-shan

clutch
greimeire
gruhm-er-uh

exhaust system
seol traoghaidh
shawl trao-y

cylinder
siolandair
seel-and-er

fan belt
crios gaotharain
krees gao-har-en

disc brake
breic clair
brek claar

foot pump
pumpa coise
pum-puh kosh-uh

distributor
compairtear
com-pars-jer

fuse
fius
fews

door
doras
dor-as

fuel pump
pumpa connaidh
pum-puh koen-y

Car parts

fuel guage
tomhas connaidh
*taw-as **koen**-y*

gear box
gior-bhocsa
*keer-**vok**-suh*

gear lever
gior shlat
*keer **hlat***

generator
gineadair
***keen**-ad-er*

hammer
ord
awrsd

hand brake
breic laimh
*brek **liev***

hazard lights
solais eiginn
***sol**-ish **ayk**-ing*

headlights
solais mhora
***sol**-ish **voer**-uh*

hood
mullach
***mul**-ach*

horn
dudach
***tood**-ach*

hose
piob
peeb

ignition
adhnadh
***aon**-ugh*

ignition key
iuchair adhnaidh
*yuch-er **aon**-y*

indicator
taisbeanair
*tash-**ben**-er*

jack
seac
shachk

lights
solais
***sol**-ish*

125

Car parts

lock
glas
glas

oil
ola
ol-uh

oil filter
siolan ola
shee-lan ol-uh

oil pressure
neart ola
nyarst ol-uh

petrol
peatrol
pet-rol

points
goban
kohb-uhn

pump
pumpa
pum-puh

radiator
reideadair
rayj-ad-er

rear-view mirror
sgathan cuil
skaa-han cool

reflectors
dearrsain
jaar-sen

reversing light
solais tillidh
sol-ish jeel-y

roof rack
cliabh mhullaich
clee-iv vul-ich

screwdriver
sgriubhaire
screw-er-uh

seat
suidheachan
suy-ach-an

seat belt
crios shuidheachain
krees huy-ach-en

shock absorber
socrachan
sok-rach-an

Car parts

silencer
muchair
mooch-er

socket set
socaidean
sok-ej-uhn

spanner
spanair
span-er

spare part
pairt eiginn
parsj ayk-ing

spark plug
sradaire
strad-er-uh

speedometer
astar-chleoc
asd-er-chlochk

starter motor
inneal spreigidh
een-yal spraik-y

steering
stiuireadh
stew-rugh

steering wheel
cuibhle stiuiridh
cuy-luh stew-ry

stoplight
solas stad
sol-as stad

sun roof
fosglan greine
fosk-lan gray-nuh

suspension
fo-chrochadh
foh-chroch-ugh

tools
innealan
een-yal-uhn

towbar
ball-tarraing
bowl-tar-ing

transmission
tar-chur
tar-chur

trunk
ciste
keesh-juh

Car parts

tyre
taidhear
tie-ir

warning light
solas rabhaidh
sol-as rav-y

wheels
cuibhlichean
cuy-lich-uhn

windscreen
uinneag aghaidh
un-yak ugh-y

windscreen wipers
suatharain
soo-a-har-en

wrench
glamair
glaam-er

EATING OUT

The Highlands offer a variety of options for eating out, ranging from hotel dining-rooms to restaurants and small pubs. As might be expected, the choice is greater in larger towns and villages than in rural areas, though even in remote spots one may find a pub or restaurant highly commended for its food. Bar meals, whether in a hotel or pub, tend to be popular at lunchtime – traditionally between 12 noon and 2pm, though an increasing number of pubs now offer an all-day snacks and meals service. In towns some restaurants offer a set "businessman's" lunch at competitive prices. On main routes one may find transport cafes and eating facilities at service stations, though again they are fewer in the remoter areas.

Local people tend to take their main meal of the day in the early evening and the tourist industry broadly conforms to this pattern. While Scotland's major cities offer late-night eating facilities, most hotels and pubs in the Highlands like to take their last orders for food before 9pm. Restaurants may stay open slightly later, some of them until midnight, especially Indian and Chinese restaurants which can be found in most towns. "Take-away" facilities are also usually open until around 11pm or midnight.

Reservations

In some districts with a tradition of Sabbath observance –
mainly the islands of Lewis and Harris and some communities on the north-west mainland – eating facilities may be
restricted on a Sunday. For residents in hotels or B & B
establishments this should present no problem, but those
who are self-catering or camping should ascertain beforehand what is available.

Reservations

Should we reserve a table?
Am bu choir dhuinn bord a ghleidheadh?
*Uhm bu **chawr** yeen **bawrsd** uh **ghlay**-ugh?*

Can I book a table for four at 8 o'clock?
Faod mi bord a ghleidheadh son ceathrar aig ochd uairean?
*Faod mee bawrsd uh **ghlay**-ugh son **ker**-uhr ek ochk **oo-ar-
uhn**?*

Can we have a table for four?
Faod sinn bord fhaighinn son ceathrar?
*Faod sheen **bawrsd** ie-ing son **ker**-uhr?*

I am a vegetarian
Glasraich bhios mi ag ithe
***Glas**-rich vees mee geech-uh*

We would like a table by the window
Chordadh bord ruinn ris an uinneig
***Chawrs**-dugh **bawrsd** reen reesh uhn **un**-yek*

Useful questions

We would like a table on the terrace
Chordadh bord ruinn air a' bharraid
Chawrs-dugh bawrsd reen air uh var-ej

Useful questions

Are vegetables included?
Bheil glasraich comhla ris?
Vail glas-rich caw-luh reesh?

Do you have a local speciality?
Bheil biadh araid dhan aite agaibh?
Vail bee-ugh aar-ij ghan aaj ak-iv?

Do you have a set menu?
Bheil cairt steidhichte agaibh?
Vail carsd shtay-ich-juh ak-iv?

What do you recommmend?
De mholadh sibh?
Jay vol-ugh sheev?

What is the dish of the day?
De biadh an latha?
Jay bee-ugh uhn laa?

What is the soup of the day?
De brot an latha?
Jay brot uh laa?

Useful questions

What is this called?
De chanas sibh ri seo?
*Jay **chan**-is sheev ree sho?*

What is this dish like?
Co ris tha seo coltach?
*Coh **reesh** ha sho **cohl**-ach?*

What wine do you recommend?
De am fion a mholadh sibh?
*Jay uhm **fee**-uhn uh **vol**-ugh sheev?*

Do you have fruit?
Bheil measan agaibh?
*Vail **mees**-uhn ak-iv?*

How do I eat this?
Ciamar dh'itheas mi seo?
*Cya-mar **yeech**-is mee sho?*

Is this wine good?
Bheil am fion seo math?
*Vail uhm **fee**-uhn sho ma?*

Is this cheese very strong?
Bheil an caise seo gle laidir?
*Vail uhn **caash**-uh sho **glay laj**-ir?*

Is this good?
Bheil seo math?
*Vail sho **ma**?*

Useful questions

What is this?
De seo?
Jay sho?

Do you have fish?
Bheil iasg agaibh?
Vail ee-isk ak-iv?

What sort of fish do you have?
De seorsa iasg a th'agaibh?
Jay shawrs ee-isk uh hak-iv?

What sort of meat do you have?
De seorsa feol a th'agaibh?
*Jay shawrs-uh **fyawl** uh hak-iv?*

Is the fish freshly caught?
Bheil an t-iasg air ur-ghlacadh?
*Vail uhn **jee-isk** air **oor-ghlak**-ugh?*

What is black pudding?
De th'ann am marag dhubh?
*Jay hown uhm mar-ak **ghu**?*

Do you have shellfish?
Bheil maorach agaibh?
*Vail **maor**-ach ak-iv?*

133

Ordering your meal

Ordering your meal

The menu, please
An clar-bidh, le'r toil
Uhn claar-bee, lair tol

I will take the set menu
Gabhaidh mis an clar steidhichte
*Gav-y meesh uhn claar **shtay-ich-juh***

Can we start with soup?
Faod sinn toiseachadh le brot?
*Faod sheen **tawsh**-ach-uh lai **brot?***

   I like my steak — very rare
Is toigh leam staoig — gle amh
   *Iss tie lum stayk — **glay** aff*

               — rare
               — amh
               — *aff*

               — medium rare
               — meadhonach amh
               — ***mee**-an-och aff*

               — well done
               — gle bhruich
               — ***glay** vreech*

134

Ordering your meal

Could we have some butter?
Faod sinn im fhaighinn?
*Faod sheen **eem** ie-ing?*

We need some bread, please
Tha feum againn air aran, le'r toil
*Haa **faym** ak-ing air **ar**-an, lair tol*

I will have salad
Gabhaidh mi sailead
*Gav-y mee **sal**-ad*

I will take that
Gabhaidh mi sin
Gav-y mee sheen

That is for me
Tha sin dhomh-sa
*Haa sheen **ghaw**-suh*

Could we have some more bread, please
Faigh sinn tuilleadh arain, le'r toil
*Fie sheen **teel**-yuh ar-en, lair tol*

Can I see the menu again, please
Faic mi an clar a ris, le'r toil
*Fiek mee uhn claar uh **reesh**, lair tol*

Can I have the salt?
Faigh mi an salann?
*Fie mee uhn **sal**-in?*

135

Food

Food

The traditional Highland diet depended on local produce, plainly cooked. Given that most of the population were crofters, farmers or fishermen they bred, grew or fished for their own food supply. There were times of poverty and dearth, of couse, particularly in the mid-nineteenth century, but in good years they could enjoy a satisifying variety of food. They bred their own beef and mutton, they produced their own dairy produce, they grew their own crops of oats, barley and potatoes, and they asserted a traditional right to take a deer from the hill or a salmon from the river (or even distil their own whisky) whatever the law might say. And the western seas provided the islanders and the coastal dwellers with a rich variety of fresh fish which could be preserved by salting, drying or smoking.

The best Highland hotels and restaurants – and many of them have earned prestigious culinary awards – build their menus around these same basic ingredients. They pride themselves on the excellence of their home-bred beef and mutton, on the richness of their local venison and salmon, and on the freshness of their seafood. In west coast restaurants the prawns and lobster that grace the evening dinner plates were still in the sea that morning. And to the basic traditional produce most eating establishments add a selection of international dishes to meet the varies tastes of an international tourist clientele.

Food

Traditionally, Highland hotel menus were couched in English (or indeed sometimes in French) and largely still are. But with the reviving popularity Gaelic some establishments use that language as well. The following basic list should be of help.

adag
ad-ack
haddock

bairnich
baar-nich
limpets

bradan
brat-an
salmon

breac
brechk
trout

brot
brot
vegetable soup

buntata
puhn-aat-uh
potatoes

cal
caal
cabbage

cal-duileasg
caal-dil-isk
dulse (seaweed) soup

cal-gruthach
caal-gru-ach
cauliflower

cearc-fhrangach
kyark-rang-ach
turkey

cearc-fhraoich
kyark-raoch
grouse

coilleagain
cuhl-yak-en
cockles

137

Food

crubagan
croop-ack-an
crabs

currain
cur-en
carrots

easag
ays-ack
pheasant

eisirean
ai-shir-in
oysters

feoil
fyawl
meat

fiasgain
fee-ask-en
mussels

giomaich Lochlannaich
gyum-ich-loch-lan-ich
prawns

giomaich
gyum-ich
lobsters

glasraich
glas-rich
vegetables

iasg
ee-isk
fish

iasg geal
ee-isk-gyal
white fish

iasg saillte
ee-isk-siel-juh
salt fish

langa
lang-uh
ling

maorach
maor-ach
shellfish

marag-dhubh
mar-ack-ghu
black pudding (a savoury
sausage)

marag-gheal
mar-ack-yal
white pudding (similar)

Food

mart-fheoil
marsd-yawl
beef

measan
mees-uhn
fruit

muc-fheoil
muchk-yawl
pork

mult-fheoil
mult-yawl
lamb

oraindsearan
or-enj-er-uhn
oranges

peasair
pais-er
peas

peuran
pay-ruhn
pears

ponair
pawn-er
beans

rionnach
run-ach
mackerel

sgadan
skat-an
herring

sitheann-circe
shee-uhn-keerk
chicken

sitheann-fheidh
shee-uhn-ay
venison

sneap
shnayp
turnip

subh-lair
su-laar
strawberry

suibheag
su-ack
raspberry

trosg
trosk
cod

Ordering drinks

tunnag
tun-ack
duck

ubhlan
ool-uhn
apples

Ordering drinks

The wine list, please
An clar fion, le'r toil
Uhn claar feen, lair tol

We will take the Rioja
Gabhaidh sinn an Rioja
Gav-y sheen uhn Rioja

A bottle of house red wine, please
Botal de dh'fhion dearg an taighe, le'r toil
Bot-il de yeen jer-ak uhn tie-uh, lair tol

A glass of dry white wine, please
Glainne de dh'fhion geal tioram, le'r toil
Glan-yuh de yeen gyal jeer-im, lair tol

Another bottle of red wine, please
Botal eile de dh'fhion dearg, le'r toil
Bot-il ail-uh de yeen jer-ak, lair tol

Ordering drinks

Another glass, please
Glainne eile, le'r toil
Glan-yuh ail-uh, alir tol

Black coffee, please
Cofaidh dubh, le'r toil
Cof-y du, lair tol

Can we have some (still/sparkling) mineral water?
Faigh sinn uisge iarainn (balbh/beo)?
Fie sheen eesh-guh eer-ing (bal-iv/ byaw)?

Coffee with milk, please
Cofaidh is bainne, le'r toil
Cof-y iss ban-yuh, lair tol

Some plain water, please
Uisge fuar, le'r toil
Eesh-guh foo-ar, lair tol

Two beers, please
Da leann, le'r toil
Daa lyoon, lair tol

branndaidh
brown-y
brandy

Drinks

Drinks

deoch
joch
drink

fion dearg
*fee-uhn-**jer**-ack*
red wine

fion geal
*fee-uhn-**gyal***
white wine

leann
lyoon
beer

ruma
***rum**-uh*
rum

sineabhar
*shin-**ay**-ver*
gin

uisge-beatha
*ish-gyi-**be**-uh*
whisky

Paying the bill

Can we have the bill, please
Faigh sinn an cunntas, le'r toil
*Fie sheen uhn **coon**-das, lair tol*

Is service included?
Bheil.seirbhis ann?
*Vail **shair**-iv-ish own?*

Complaints and compliments

Is there any extra charge?
Bheil cosgais a bharrachd ann?
*Vail **cosg-ish** uh **var**-achk own?*

I haven't enough money
Chan eil airgiod gu leoir agam
*Chan ail **er**-ik-uhd gu lyawr ak-am*

This is not correct
Chan eil seo ceart
Chan ail sho cyarst

This not my bill
Chan e seo mo chunntas-sa
*Chan e sho moh **choon**-das-uh*

You have given me the wrong change
Tha sibh air an iomlaid chearr thoirt dhomh
*Haa sheev air uhn **yum**-lej chyaar horst gho*

Complaints and compliments

This is cold
Tha seo fuar
Haa sho foo-ar

This is not what I ordered
Chan e seo a dh'ordaich mi
*Chan e sho uh **ghawrd**-ich mee*

143

Complaints and compliments

Waiter! We have been waiting for a long time
Ille! Tha sinn air a bhith feitheamh greis
*Eel-yuh! Haa sheen air uh vee **fay-hiv** **graish***

Can I have the recipe?
Faigh mi am modh?
Fie mee uhm moh?

The meal was excellent
Bha am biadh air leth
Vaa uhm bee-ugh air lai

This is excellent
Tha seo air leth math
Haa sho air lai ma

OUT AND ABOUT

The weather

The weather in the Highlands can be both unpredictable and localised. It is perfectly possible to have a raging gale from the Atlantic on the west coast and a mild, warm day on the east coast, or vice versa. Warmed by the waters of the Gulf Stream the west coast generally enjoys a mild, moist climate, though the low-lying island of Tiree frequently breaks British records for all-day sunshine. Equally, the low glens of the central Highlands may enjoy fine summer weather while the high plateau of the neighbouring Cairngorms suffers from wind-chill of Arctic intensity.

In such circumstances hill-walkers particularly should be adequately equipped. They should be well-shod at all times, and even on the finest summer day they should carry enough bad-weather clothing to cope with a sudden change. They should also leave a message at base ourlining their proposed route and time of return or arrival at their next destination. Every year the rescue services waste endless time locating ill-equipped hill-walkers who have got into trouble.

Radio and television carry frequent weather forecasts but it can be difficult for them to predict localised conditions.

The weather

Is it going to get any warmer?
Bheil e dol a dh'fhas nas blaithe?
*Vail e dol uh ghaas nas **blaa**-yuh?*

Is it going to stay like this?
Fan e mar seo?
Fan e mar sho?

Is there going to be a thunderstorm?
Bheil tairneanaich gu bhith ann?
*Vail **taarn**-yan-ich gu vee own?*

Isn't it a lovely day?
Nach breagh an la a th'ann?
*Nach **bree-a** uhn laa uh hown?*

It has stopped snowing
Tha e air stad a chur
Haa e air stad uh chur

It is a very clear night
Tha an oidhche gle shoilleir
*Haa uhn **iech**-yuh glay **huhl**-ir*

It is far too hot
Tha e fada ro theth
*Haa e **fad-uh** ro **hai***

It is foggy
Tha ceo ann
Haa cyaw own

146

The weather

It is raining again
Tha e sileadh a ris
*Haa e **sheel**-ugh uh reesh*

It is very cold
The e gle fhuar
*Haa e glay **oo**-ar*

It is very windy
Tha gaoth laidir ann
*Haa gao **laa**-jir own*

There is a cool breeze
Tha oiteag fhionnar ann
*Haa oj-ak **yun**-ar own*

What is the temperature?
De an teas a th'ann?
*Jay uhn **jais** uh hown?*

Is it going to be — fine?
  Bheil e gu bhith — breagha?
  *Vail e gu vee — **bree**-a*

  — windy?
  — gaothar
  *— **gao**-har*

  — rainy?
  — fliuch
  — flewch

147

On the beach

Is it going to be snowy?
Bheil e gu bhith a' cur?
Vail e gu vee uh cur

Will it be cold tonight?
Am bi e fuar an nochd?
*Uhm bee e **foo**-ar uhn nochk?*

Will the weather improve?
Am fas an side nas fhearr?
*Uhm faas uhn **shee**-juh nas yaar?*

Will the wind die down?
An socraich a' ghaoth?
*Uhn **soc**-rich uh ghao?*

On the beach

Can we change here?
Faod sinn cur dhinn an seo?
Faod sheen cur yeen uhn sho?

Can you recommend a quiet beach?
Am mol; thu trsigh shamhach?
*Uhm mol oo **traa**-yuh **haav**-ach?*

Is it safe to swim here?
Bheil e sabhailte snamh an seo?
*Vail e **saav**-il-juh **snaav** uhn sho?*

148

On the beach

Is the current strong?
Bheil an sruth laidir?
Vail uhn stru laa-jir?

Is the sea calm?
Bheil feath ann?
Vail fee-a own?

> **Can I rent — a sailing boat?**
> Faod mi — bata siuil fhasdadh?
> *Faod mee — bat-uh shool asd-ugh?*

> > **— a rowing boat?**
> > — bata raimh fhasdadh?
> > *— bat-uh raav asd-ugh?*

Is it possible to go — sailing?
Bheil e comasach — seoladh?
Vail e cohm-as-ac — shawl-ugh?

> > **— surfing?**
> > — copadh?
> > *— cohp-ugh?*

> > **— water skiing?**
> > — sgitheadh uisge?
> > *— sgee-ugh eesh-guh?*

> > **— wind surfing?**
> > — copadh gaoithe?
> > *— cohp-ugh gao-hugh?*

149

Sport and recreation

Is the water warm?
Bheil an t-uisge blath?
Vail uhn teesh-guh blaa?

Is there a heated smimming pool?
Bheil an t-amar snamh teasaichte
Vail uhn tam-ar snaav jais-ich-juh?

Is there a lifeguard here?
Bheil fear-faire an seo?
Vail fer-far uhn sho?

Is this beach private?
Bheil an traigh seo diomhair?
Vail uhn traa-yuh sho jee-vir?

When is high tide?
Cuin a tha muir lan ann?
Cun uh haa mur laan own?

When is low tide?
Cuin a tha muir traigh ann?
Cun uh haa mur traa-yuh own?

Sport and recreation

Can I rent the equipment?
Faod mi an acfhainn fhasdadh?
Faod mee uhn achk-in asd-ugh?

Entertainment

Can we go riding?
Faod sinn marcachd?
*Faod sheen **mark**-achk?*

Faod sinn cluich — tennis?
Faod sinn cluich — cneutag?
*Faod sheen clich — **crait**-ag?*

— golf?
— goilf?
— goilf?

— volleyball?
— ball-duirn?
*— ball-**doorn?***

Where can we fish?
Caite faod sinn iasgach?
*Caa-juh faod sheen **ee-ask**-ach?*

Do we need a permit?
Feum sinn cead?
*Faym sheen **kyait?***

Entertainment

How much is it for a child?
De tha e son leanabh?
*Jay haa e son **len**-iv?*

151

Entertainment

How much is it per person?
De tha e an urra?
*Jay haa e uhn **ur**-uh?*

How much is it to get in?
Jay haa e faighinn astigh?
*Jay haa e fie-ing uh-**stie**?*

> **Is there — a disco?**
> Bheil — disco ann?
> *Vail — disco own?*

> > **— a good night-club?**
> > — deagh chlub-oidhche ann?
> > *— jay chluhb-**iech**-uh own?*

> > **— a theatre?**
> > — taigh-cluich ann?
> > *— tie-**clich** own?*

Are there any films in English?
Bheil filmichean Beurla ann?
*Vail **film**-ich-uhn **Bayr**-luh own?*

Two stall tickets, please?
Da bhileag staile, le'r toil?
*Daa veel-ag -**staal**-uh, lair tol?*

Is there a reduction for children?
Bheil e nas saoire son clann?
*Vail e nas **saor**-uh son clown?*

Sightseeing

Are there any boat trips on the river?
Bheil tursan bhata air an abhainn?
*Vail **tur**-suhn vaa-tuh air uhn **av**-in?*

Are there any guideadh tours of the castle?
Bheil cuairtean fo threoir aig a' chaisteal?
*Vail **coo-ars**-juhn foh hrawr ek uh **chash**-jal?*

Are there any guided tours?
Vail cuairtean fo threoir ann?
*Vail **coo-ars**-juhn foh hrawr own?*

What is there to see?
De tha ri fhaicinn?
*Jay haa ree **iechk**-in?*

What is this building?
De an togalach a tha seo?
*Jay uhn **tohk**-al-acj uh haa sho?*

When was it built?
Cuin a thogadh e?
*Cun uh **hohk**-ugh e?*

Is it open to the public?
Bheil e fosgailte dhan mhor-shluagh?
*Vail e **fosg**-il-juh ghan **voer**-hloo-ugh?*

153

Sightseeing

What is the admission charge?
De tha e faighinn astigh?
*Jay haa e **fie**-one uh-**stie**?*

Can we go in?
Faod sinn dhol astigh?
*Faod sheen ghol uh-**stie**?*

Can we go to the top?
Faod sinn dhol dhan mhullach?
*Faod sheen ghol ghan **vul**-ach?*

Can I take photos?
Faod mi dealbhan a thogail?
*Faod mee **jal**-vin uh **hohk**-el?*

Can I use flash?
Faod mi lasair a chleachdadh?
*Faod mee **las**-er uh **chleck**-ugh?*

How long does the tour take?
De cho fad's a bheir a' chuairt?
*Jay cho fats uh vair uh **choo**-arsj?*

Is there a guide book?
Bheil leabhar treoir ann?
*Vail lyawr **trawr** own*

Is there a tour of the cathedral?
Bheil cuairt dhen ard–eaglais ann?
*Vail **coo-arsj** yen aard-**aik**-lish own?*

154

Souvenirs

Is there an English-speaking guide?
Bheil neach-treoir le Beurla ann?
*Vail nyech-**trawr** lai **Bayr**-luh own?*

Is this the best view?
An e seo an sealladh as fhearr?
*Uhn e sho uhn **shal**-ugh as **yaar**?*

What time does the gallery open?
Cuin a dh'fhosglas an gailearaidh?
*Cun uh ghosg-las uhn **gal**-er-y?*

When is the bus tour?
Cuin a tha cuairt a' bhus ann?
*Cun uh haa **coo-arsj** uh vuhs own?*

Souvenirs

Have you got an English guide book?
Bheil leabhar treoir Beurla agaibh?
*Vail lyawr-**trawr** Bayr-luh **ak**-iv?*

Have you got any coloour slides?
Bheil dealbhan dathte agaibh?
*Vail jal-iv-in **daj**-uh **ak**-iv?*

Where can I buy postcards
Caite an ceannaich mi cairtean-puist?
***Caa**-juh uhn **cyan**-ich mee carsj-uhn-**pushj**?*

Going to church

Where can we buy souvenirs?
Caite an ceannaich sinn cuimhneachain?
*Caa-juh uhn **cyan**-ich mee **cuy**-nach-en?*

Going to church

In most areas of the Highland a variety of Presbyterian churches can be found while the Catholic church predominates in some districts. Methodist, Baptist and Episcopal churches can also be found in some towns. On the west coast and the islands worship is held in Gaelic as well as English. All the churches welcome visitors to their services.

Where is the — Catholic church?
Caite bheil — an eaglais Chaitligeach?
*Caa-juh vail — uhn aik-lish **Chat**-lig-ach?*

— Baptist church?
— an eaglais Bhaisteach?
*— uhn aik-lish **Vasht**-ach?*

— mosque?
— am mosc?
— uhm mosc?

— Protestant church?
— an eaglais Phrostanach?
*— uhn aik-lish **Fraws**-dan-ach?*

156

Going to church

Where is the — synagogue?
Caite bheil — an sinagog?
Caa-juh vail — uhn shin-ag-og?

What time is mass?
De an uair aig am bheil an aifhrionn?
Jay uhn oo-ar ek uhm vail uhn ier-uhn?

I would like to see — a priest
Bu thoigh leam bruidheann ri – sagart
*Bu hie lum **bree**-in ree – **sack**-art*

— a minister
— ministear
— ***meen**-ish-jer*

— a rabbi
— rabaidh
— ***rab**-ie*

SHOPPING

Supermarkets are now found in most sizeable towns in the Highlands and most groceries and foodstuffs are bought there. Only in small, remote communities is a traditional village grocery store to be found, though specialised shops such as butchers, bakers, electrical stores, clothiers, chemists and newsagents are still found in many towns.

Most supermarkets open at 8am on weekdays (9am on Sundays) and close at various times between 6pm and 10pm on different days. In large towns a few remain open over 24 hours, as do some shops attached to service stations. Local shops tend to open from 9 or 9.30am until 5.30pm, and some of them still follow the tradition of closing for one afternoon mid-week. All shops close for a day or two both at Christmas and New Year, and some observe other local holidays.

General phrases and requests

How much does that cost?
De tha sin a' cosg?
Jay haa sheen uh cosg?

158

General phrases and requests

How much is it — per kilo?
De tha e — an cile?
Jay haa e — uhn keel-uh

— per metre
— am meadair
— uhm meet-er

How much is this?
De tha seo a' cosg?
Jay haa sho uh cosg?

Have you got anything cheaper?
Bheil dad nas saoire agaibh?
*Vail dat nas **saor**-uh **ak**-iv?*

Can I see that umbrella?
Faic mi an sgailean ud?
***Fiek** mee uhn **skaal**-an uhd?*

No, the other one
Chan e, am fear eile
*Chan e, uhm fer **ail**-uh*

Can you deliver it to my hotel?
An toir sibh e gu'm taigh-osda?
*Uhn dawr sheev e gum **hie-aws**-duh?*

I do not like it
Cha toigh leam e
*Cha **tie** lum e*

159

General phrases and requests

I like this one
Is toigh leam am fear seo
*Iss **tie** lum am **fer** sho*

    I will take — this one
    Gabhaidh mi — am fear seo
    Gav-y mee — uhm fer sho

        — that one
        — am fear ud
        — uhm fer uhd

        — the other one
        — am fear eile
        — uhm fer ail-uh

        — that one over there
        — am fear ud thall
        — uhm fer ud howl

    Can I have — a carrier bag?
    Faigh mi — poca giulain?
    Fie mee — pohk-uh gew-len?

        — a receipt?
        — cuidhteas?
        — cuy-jas?

        — an itemised bill?
        — cunntas mionaideach?
        — cun-das meen-ej-ach?

General phrases and requests

Can I pay for air insurance?
Faod mi urras adhair a phaigheadh?
*Faod mee **ur**-as **a**-ir uh **faa**-yugh?*

What is the total?
De th'ann air fad?
Jay hown air fat?

Do you accept travellers' cheques?
Bheil sibh a' gabhail seicean-siubhail?
*Vail sheev uh gav-el shaic-uhn-**shoo**-il?*

I do not have enough currency
Chan eil gu leoir cuinneadh agam
*Chan ail gu lyawr **coon**-yuh **ak**-am*

I do not have enough money
Chan eil gu leoir airgead agam
*Chan ail gu lyawr **er**-ik-ad **ak**-am*

I would like to pay with my credit card
Bu thoigh leam paigheadh le mo chairt-chreideis
*Bu hie lum **paa**-yugh lai moh charst-**chraij**-ish*

Please forward a receipt to this address
Cuir an cuidhteas dhan t-seoladh seo, le'r toil
*Cur uhn **cuy**-jas ghan **tyawl**-ugh sho, lair tol*

Please wrap it up for me
Comhdaich dhomh e, le'r toil
***Caw**-dich gho e, lair tol*

161

Buying groceries

There is no need to wrap it
Chan eil feum air comhdach
*Chan ail **faym** air **caw**-dach*

Please pack this for shipment
Paisg seo son a ghiulain, le'r toil
*Pashk sho son uh **yew**-len, lair tol*

Will you send it by air freight?
An cuir sibh le plean e?
Uhn cur sheev le playn e?

Buying groceries

We need to buy some food
Feumaidh sinn biadh a cheannach
***Faym**-y sheen **bee**-ugh uh **chyan**-ach*

    I would like — a kilo of potatoes
    Bu thoigh leam — cile bhuntata
    *Bu **hie** lum — **keel**-uh **vun**-taad-uh*

        — a bar of chocolate
        — bar teoclaid
        *— baar **tyaw**-clet*

        — 100g of ground coffee
        — ceud gram cofaidh pronn
        *— **kee**-ad gram **cof**-y prown*

Buying groceries

I would like — two steaks
Bu thoigh leam — da staoig
*Bu **hie** lum — daa stayk*

— five slices of ham
— coig sliseagan hama
*— **coh-ik shleesh**-ak-uhn **ham**-uh*

— half a dozen eggs
— leth-dusan ugh
*— **lai**-dus-an **ugh***

— half a kilo of butter
— leth-chile ime
*— **lai**-cheel-uh **eem**-uh*

Can I have — some sugar, please?
Faigh mi — siucar, le'r toil?
*Fie mee — **shew**-car, lair tol?*

— a bottle of wine, please?
— botal fion, le'r toil?
*— bot-al **fee**-uhn, lair tol?*

— a kilo of sausages, please?
— cile isbeanan, le'r toil?
*— **keel**-uh **eesh**-ban-uhn, lair tol?*

— a leg of lamb, please?
— ceathramh uain, le'r toil?
*— **ker**-iv **oo**-en, lair tol?*

Groceries

Can I have a litre of milk, please?
Faigh mi liotair bainne, le'r toil?
*Fie mee lee-ter **ban**-yuh, lair tol?*

Groceries

baby food
biadh leanabh
*bee-ugh **len**-iv*

cream
uachdar
oo-ach-gar

biscuits
briosgaidean
***brees**-gej-uhn*

eggs
uighean
oo-yuhn

bread
aran
***ar**-an*

flour
min-fhlur
*meen-**loor***

butter
im
eem

jam
silidh
***sheel**-y*

cheese
caise
***caa**-shuh*

margarine
margarain
***mar**-gar-en*

coffee
cofaidh
***cof**-y*

milk
bainne
***ban**-yuh*

164

Meat and fish

mustard
mustard
mus-dart

soup
brot
brot

oil
ola
ol-uh

sugar
siucar
shew-car

pepper
piobair
peeb-er

tea
ti
tee

rice
rus
ruhs

vinegar
fion-geur
fee-uhn-gayr

salt
salann
sal-in

yoghurt
iogart
yawg-art

Meat and fish

beef
mart-fheoil
marst-yawl

fish
iasg
ee-isg

cod
trosg
trosk

herring
sgadan
scat-an

chicken
cearc
cyark

ham
hama
ham-uh

kidneys
airnean
aarn-yuhn

mussels
feusgain
fee-as-gen

165

At the newsagent's

lamb	**pork**
uan	muc-fheoil
oo-an	*muc-yawl*
liver	**sole**
gruthan l	eabag
groo-an lee-ap-ak	
meat	**veal**
feoil	laoigh-fheoil
fyawl	*laogh-yawl*

At the newsagent's

Most communities have a local newsagent, and newspapers are also available at the larger railway stations, and at supermarkets and roadside service stations. During the summer tourist season a few of the larger outlets have a selection of continental newspapers in the major European languages.

> **Do you sell — English paperbacks?**
> Bheil sibh a' reic — leabhraichean bog-chomhdach
> Beurla?
> *Vail sheev uh raik — lyawr-ich-uhn **bohk-chaw-dach**
> **Bayr-luh**?*

> **— postcards?**
> — cairtean puist?
> *— **cars**-juhn **pooshj**?*

166

At the newsagent's

Do you sell — a local map?
Bheil sibh a' reic — map ionadail?
*Vail sheev uh raik — map **een-ad-el**?*

— a road map?
— map rathaid?
*— map **raw-ij**?*

— coloured pencils?
— peansailean dathte?
*— **pen**-sel-uhn **da-juh**?*

— drawing paper?
— paipear dealbh?
*— **pie**-per **dyal-iv**?*

— felt pens?
— pinn olainn?
*— **peen ol-in**?*

I would like some postage stamps
Bu thoigh leam stampaichean
*Bu hie lum **stamp**-ich-uhn*

Do you have — English books?
Bheil — leabhraichean Beurla agaibh?
*Vail — **lyawr**-ich-uhn **Bayr**-luh **ak-iv**?*

— English newspapers?
— paipearan-naidheachd Beurla agaibh?
*— **pie**-per-uhn-**nie**-achk **Bayr**-luh **ak-iv**?*

At the tobacconist's

I need — some writing paper
Feumaidh mi — paipear sgriobhaidh
***Faym**-y mee — **pie**-per **skreev**-y*

— a bottle of ink
— botal de dhubh
— ***bot**-al dye ghu*

— a pen
— peann
— *pyown*

— a pencil
— peansail
— ***pen**-sel*

— some adhesive tape
— teip tathaidh
— *taip **taa**-hy*

— some envelopes
—ceisean litreach
— ***kay**-shan **leet**-rach*

At the tobacconist's

Do you have — cigarette papers?
Bheil — paipearan toitean agaibh?
*Vail — **pie**-per-uhn **toj**-uhn **ak**-iv?*

168

At the tobacconist's

Do you have — a box of matches?
     Bheil — bocsa lasraichean agaibh?
     Vail — boc-sa las-rich-uhn ak-iv?

        — a cigar?
        — siogar agaibh?
        — see-gar ak-iv?

        — a cigarette lighter?
        — lasadair thoitean agaibh?
        — las-ad-er hoj-uhn ak-iv?

        — a gas (butane) refill?
        — ath-lionadh gas agaibh?
        — a-leen-ugh gas ak-iv?

        — a pipe?
        — piob agaibh?
        — peeb ak-iv?

        — a pouch of pipe tobacco?
        — spliuchan tombaca pioba agaibh?
        — splew-chan tom-bac-uh peeb-uh ak-iv?

        — a pipe cleaner?
        — glanadair phiob agaibh?
        — glan-ad-er feeb ak-iv?

Have you got — any American brands?
     Bheil — seorsa Aimearaganach agaibh?
     Vail — shawrs Am-er-ag-an-ach akiv?

At the chemist's

Have you got — any English brands?
Bheil — seorsa Sasannach agaibh?
*Vail — shawrs-uh **Sas**-an-ach **ak**-iv?*

— rolling tobacco?
— tombaca suathaidh agaibh?
*— tom-**bac**-uh **soo**-hy **ak**-iv?*

A packet of . . . please
Pacaid de . . . le'r toil
Pac-ej y . . . lair tol

. . . with filter tips
. . . le barr siolaidh
*. . . lai baar **shee**-al-y*

. . . without filter tips
. . . gun barr siolaidh
*. . . gun baar **shee**-al-y*

At the chemist's

Most towns have a local chemist open during normal shopping hours. Supermarkets and service stations also usually carry a basic range of medicines, toiletries and cosmetics.

Do you have toothpaste?
Bheil uachdar fhiaclan agaibh?
*Vail **oo**-ach-kar ee-ak-luhn **ak**-iv?*

At the chemist's

I need some high-protection suntan cream
Feumaidh mi uachdar greine laidir
Fay-my mee oo-ach-kar gray-nuh laa-jir

Can you give me something for **— a headache?**
   An toir sibh dhomh rud air son   — ceann goirt?
   Uhn dawr sheev gho rut air son   — *cyown gorshj?*

                                 — insect bites?
                                 — bideadh bhiastag?
                                 — *bee-juh vee-as-dak?*

                                 — a cold?
                                 — cnatan?
                                 — *crat-an?*

                                 — a cough?
                                 — casad?
                                 — *cas-uhd?*

                                 — a sore throat?
                                 — amhach ghoirt?
                                 — *av-ach ghorshj?*

                                 — an upset stomach?
                                 — stamag ghoirt?
                                 — *stam-ak ghorshj?*

                                 — toothache?
                                 — an deididh?
                                 — *uhn jay-jy?*

Medicines and toiletries

Can you give me something for — hay fever?
An toir sibh dhomh rud air son — fiabhras feoir?
Uhn dawr sheev gho rut air son — *fee-ras fyawr?*

— sunburn?
— losgadh greine?
— *luhsk-ugh gray-nuh?*

Do I need a prescription?
Feum mi bileag-leigh?
Faym mee beel-ak-lay?

How many do I take?
Cia-meud a ghabhas mi?
Cya-meed uh ghav-as mee?

How often do I take them?
De cho tric's a ghabhas mi iad?
Jay cho treeks uh ghav-as mee ee-ad?

Are they safe for children to take?
Bheil iad sabhailte son clann?
Vail ee-ad saav-il-juh son clown?

Medicines and toiletries

antihistamine
casg-hiostamain
cask-heest-am-en

172

Medicines and toiletries

antiseptic
casg-lobhaidh
cask-loh-y

aspirin
aspran
asp-ran

bandage
breid
brayj

bubble bath
amar cop
am-uhr cohp

cleansing milk
bainne glanaidh
ban-yuh glanb-y

conditioner
deasaichear
jay-sich-er

condom
casgan
cask-an

contraceptive
casg-gineamhainn
cask-geen-av-in

cotton wool
cotan
cot-an

deodorant
casg-failidh
cask-faal-y

disinfectant
di-ghalaran
jee-ghal-ar-an

eau de Cologne
uisge Chologne
ish-gyi Chol-on

eye shadow
faileas shuil
fal-as hool

face powder
fudar gnuis
food-ar groosh

hair spray
frasair fuilt
fras-er fulj

hand cream
uachdar laimhe
oo-ach-kar lie-vuh

Medicines and toiletries

insect repellant
casg bhiastag
cask **vee**-as-dak

laxative
purgaid
pur-ak-ej

lipstick
dath-bhile
da-veel-uh

mascara
mascara
mas-caar-a

moisturiser
taiseadair
tash-ad-er

mouthwash
sgolan-beoil
*skol-an-**byawl***

nail file
liobhan ine
*lee-van **een-uh***

nail varnish
dath ine
*da **een-uh***

nail varnish remover
glanadair dath ine
*glan-ad-er da **een-uh***

perfume
cubhrachd
coor-achk

plasters
plasdan
plaas-duhn

razor blades
faobhair rasair
*fao-her **raas-er***

sanitary towels
luideagan slainteil
*luj-ak-uhn **slaan-jel***

shampoo
siampu
*sham-**poo***

shaving cream
uachdar rasair
*oo-ach-kar **raas-er***

soap
siabann
shee-bin

Shopping for clothes

suntan lotion
cungaidh greine
cung-y gray-nuh

talc
talc
talc

tampons
stupaidean
stup-ej-uhn

tissues
neapaigean-paipeir
nep-ik-en-pie-per

toilet water
uisge cubhraidh
ish-gyi coor-y

toothpaste
uachdar fhiaclan
oo-ach-kar ee-ak-lan

Shopping for clothes

I am just looking, thank you
Chan eil mi ach a' coimhead, tapadh leibh
Chan ail mee ach uh coy-uhd, tap-uh leev

I do not like it
Cha toigh leam e
Cha tie lum e

I like it
Is toigh leam e
Iss tie lum e

I will take it
Gabhaidh mi e
Gav-y mee e

175

Shopping for clothes

I like — this one
Is toigh leam — am fear seo
Iss tie lum — uhm fer sho

— that one there
— am fear ud thall
— uhm fer uhd howl

— the one in the window
— am fear 'san uinneag
*— uhm fer san **un**-yak*

I would like — this suit
Bu thoigh leam — an deise seo
Bu hie lum — uhn jaysh-uh sho

— this hat
— an ad seo
— uhn at sho

I would like one — with a zip
Bu thoigh leam fear— le siop
Bu hie lum fer — lai sheep

— without a belt
— gun chrios
— gun chrees

Can you please measure me?
An tomhais sibh mi, le'r toil?
*Uhn **to**-ish sheev mee, lair tol?*

176

Shopping for clothes

Can I change it if it does not fit?
Faod mi atharrachadh mur am freagair e?
Faod mee a-har-ach-uh muhr uh frai-gar e mee?

Have you got this in other colours?
Bheil seo agaibh an dathan eile?
Vail sho ak-iv uhn da-han ail-uh?

I take a large shoe size
Feumaidh mi brog mhor
Fay-my mee brawk voer

I take continental size 40
Tha mi gabhail meud da fhichead Eorpach
Haa mee gav-el mayt da eech-ad yawr-pach

Is it too long?
Bheil e ro fhada?
Vail e ro at-uh?

Is it too short?
Bheil e ro ghoirid?
Vail e ro ghuhr-ij?

Is there a full-length mirror?
Bheil sgathan fada ann?
Vail skaa-han fat own?

Is this all you have?
An e seo na th'agaibh?
Uhn e sho na hak-iv?

177

Shopping for clothes

It does not fit
Chan eil e freagairt
*Chan ail e **fraik**-arj*

It does not suit me
Chan eil e tighinn rium
*Chan ail e **jeen** rum*

May I see it in daylight?
Faic mi ri solas latha e?
*Fìek mee ree sol-as **laa** e?*

Where is the changing room?
Caite bheil an seomar cur umad?
*Caa-juh vail uhn **shaw**-mar cur um-ad?*

Where can I try it on?
Caite am fiach mi orm e?
*Caa-juh uhm **fee**-ach mee or-am e?*

Have you got — a large size?
Bheil — meud mhor agaibh?
*Vail — mayt voer **ak**-iv?*

— a small size?
— meud bheag agaibh?
*— mayt vaik **ak**-iv?*

What is it made of?
Co dhe tha e deante?
*Coh **ye** haa e jee-an-tuh?*

Clothes and accessories

Is it guaranteed?
Bheil barrantas leis?
*Vail **bar**-ant-as laish?*

Will it shrink?
An teid e stigh?
*Uhn jait e **stie**?*

Is it drip-dry?
An tiormaich e crochte?
*Uhn **jeer**-am-ich e **croch**-juh?*

Is it dry-clean only?
An e glanadh tioram amhain a th'ann?
*Uhn e **glan**-uh **jeer**-am uh-**vaan** uh hown?*

Is it machine washable?
An gabh a nighe an inneal?
*Uhn gav uh **nee**-uh an **een**-yal?*

Clothes and accessories

acrylic cardigan
acriolaic cardagan
*ac-**ril**-ic **caar**-dik-an*

belt
crios
crees

179

Clothes and accessories

blouse
blabhsa
blow-suh

bra
bra
braa

bracelet
bann-duirn
bown-doorn

brooch
braisde
braash-juh

button
putan
put-an

earrings
cluas-fhail
cloo-as-aal

espadrilles
cuarain-rop
coo-ar-en-rawp

fur
bian
bee-an

gloves
meatagan
met-ak-uhn

handbag
baga-laimh
bak-a-liev

handkerchief
neapaigean
nyep-ik-an

hat
ad
at

jacket
seacaid
shech-kej

coat
cota
caw-tuh

corduroy
cord
cawrsd

cotton
cotan
cot-an

Clothes and accessories

denim
denim
den-im

necklace
crios-muineil
crees-moon-yal

dress
dreasa
dres-uh

nightdress
gun-oidhche
gun-iech-uh

dungarees
dongairidh
dong-ar-ee

nylon
naidhlean
nie-lan

jeans
dinichean
jeen-ich-uhn

pants (women's)
drathais
draa-ish

jersey
geansaidh
gen-sy

petticoat
cota-ban
caw-tuh-baan

lace
lios
lees

polyester
poilidh-astair
pol-y-asd-er

leather
leathar
lyai-hir

pullover
peitean
pai-jen

linen
anart
an-art

purse
sporan
spor-an

181

Clothes and accessories

pyjamas
trusgan-leap
trus-gan-lep

sweater
geansaidh
gen-sy

raincoat
cota-frois
caw-duh-frosh

swim trunks
briogais shnamh
breek-ish naav

ring
fainne
faan-yuh

swimsuit
trusgan snamh
trus-gan snaav

socks
mogain
mok-en

sandals
cuarain
coo-ar-en

stockings
stocainnean
stok-en-in

scarf
crabhat
cra-vat

suede
leathar-bhog
lyai-hir-vohk

shirt
leine
lay-nuh

suit (men's)
deise
jay-shuh

shoes
brogan
braw-kuhn

suit (women's)
deise
jay-shuh

shorts
briogais-ghearr
breek-ish-yaar

Clothes and accessories

silk
sioda
shee-duh

skirt
sgiort
sgyuhrt

slip
fo-chota
foh-chaw-duh

T-shirt
leine-T
lay-nuh-tee

terylene
tearalain
ter-al-en

tie
bann-amhaich
bown-av-ich

tights
stocainn-ard
stok-en-aard

towel
searadair
sher-ad-er

trousers
briogais
breek-ish

umbrella
sgailean
skaal-an

underpants (men's)
drathais
draa-ish

velvet
meileabhaid
mail-av-ej

vest
siomad
seem-id

wallet
leabhar-poc
lyaw-ar-pawk

watch
uaireadair
oo-ar-ad-er

wool
cloimh
claw-yuh

183

Photography

zip
siop
seep

Photography

I need a film — for this camera
Feumaidh mi film — son a' chamara seo
*Fay-my mee film — son uh **cham-ar-a** sho*

— for this camcorder
— son a' chamcordair seo
*— son uh **cham-cor-der** sho*

— for this cine-camera
— son uh chamara-sine seo
*— son uh cham-ar-a-**seen**-uh sho*

— for this video camera
— son a' chamara bhideo seo
*— son uh cham-ar-a **vid**-yoh sho*

Can you develop this film, please?
An nochd sibh am film seo, le'r toil?
*Uhn **nochk** sheef uhm film sho, lair tol?*

I would like this photo enlarged
Bu mhath leam an dealbh seo meudaichte
*Bu **va** lum uhn jal-iv sho **may**-dich-juh*

Camera repairs

I would like two prints of this one
Bu mhath leam da chlo dhen fhear seo
*Bu va lum **daa** chlaw yen **er** sho*

When will the photos be ready?
Cuin a bhios na dealbhan deiseil?
***Cun** uh vees na jal-vuhn jaysh-al?*

I want — a black and white film
Tha mi ag iarraidh— film dubh is geal
*Ha mee **geer**-y — film du iss **gyal***

— a colour print film
— film dathte
*— film **da**-juh*

— a colour slide film
— film soilleir dathte
*— film **suhl**-yer **da**-juh*

— batteries for the flash
— batraidhean son an lasair
*— **bat**-ree-en son uh **las**-er*

Camera repairs

I am having touble with my camera
Tha trioblaid agam le mo chamara
*Ha **treep**-lej ak-am lai moh **cham**-ar-a*

185

Camera parts

The film is jammed
Tha am film glacte
Ha uhm film glak-juh

There is something wrong with my camera
Tha rud-eigin cearr air mo chamara
Ha rud-aik-in cyaar air moh cham-ar-a

Where can I get my camera repaired?
Caite faigh mi mo chamara a charadh?
Caa-juh fie mee moh cham-ar-a chaar-ugh?

Camera parts

accessory
treallaich
tral-ich

blue filter
siolan gorm
shee-lan gor-uhm

camcorder
camcordair
cam-cord-er

cartridge
peilear
pail-er

cassette
casaid
cas-ej

cine-camera
camara-sine
cam-ar-a-sheen-uh

distance
astar
asd-er

enlargement
meudachadh
mayt-ach-ugh

186

Camera parts

exposure
nochdadh
noch-kuh

exposure meter
inneal nochdaidh
enn-yal noch-ky

flash
lasair
las-er

flash bulb
bolg lasaidh
bolg las-y

flash cube
ciub lasaidh
cup las-y

focal distance
astar amais
asd-er am-ish

focus
amas
am-iss

image
iomhaigh
ee-av-ie

in focus
ann an amas
own uhn am-iss

lens cover
ceap leansa
kep len-sa

lens
leansa
len-sa

negative
claon-chlo
cleen-chlaw

out of focus
mach a amas
mach a am-iss

over-esposed
ro-nochdte
ro-noch-juh

picture
dealbh
jal-iv

print
clo
claw

At the hairdresser's

projector
tilgeadair
jeel-ik-ad-er

slide
slaod
slaod

red filter
siolan dearg
shee-lan jer-ak

transparency
dealbh shoilleir
jal-iv huhl-yer

reel
piorna
pyur-nuh

tripod
tri-chasach
tree-chas-ach

shade
faileas
fal-iss

viewfinder
lorgan-seallaidh
lor-ak-an shal-y

shutter
comhla
caw-luh

wide-angle lens
leansa fharsaing
len-suh ars-ing

shutter speed
astar comhla
asd-er caw-luh

yellow filter
siolan buidhe
shee-lan buy-uh

At the hairdresser's

I would like to make an appointment
Bu mhath leam uair a dheanamh riut
Bu va lum oo-ar a yen-iv rut

188

At the hairdresser's

I want — a haircut
Tha mi ag iarraidh — bearradh fuilt
*Ha mee **geer-y** — **byar**-ugh **fulj***

— a trim
— sgioblachadh
— *skeep-lach-ugh*

Not too much off
Na toir cus dhe
*Na tawr **cus** ye*

Take a little more off the back
Thoir beagan a bharrachd far a' chuil
*Hawr **baik**-an uh **var**-achk far uh **chool***

Please cut my hair — short
Le'r toil, gearr m'fhalt — goirid
*Lair tol, gyaar malt — **guhr**-ij*

— fairly short
— meadhonach goirid
— ***mee**-an-ach **guhr**-ij*

— in a fringe
— le fraoidhneas
— *lai **frie**-nas*

That is fine, thank you
Tha sin glan, tapadh leibh
*Ha sheen **glan**, **tap**-uh leev*

189

At the hairdresser's

I would like — a perm
Bu mhath leam — perm
*Bu va lum — **perm***

— a blow-dry
— seideadh tioram
*— **shayd-**yugh **jeer**-am*

— my hair dyed
— m'fhalt dathte
*— malt **da**-juh*

— my hair streaked
— m'fhalt stiallach
*— malt **shtee**-al-ach*

— a shampoo and cut
— siampu is bearradh
*— sham-**poo** iss **byar**-ugh*

— a shampoo and set
— siampu is cumadh
*— sham-**poo** iss **cum**-ugh*

— a conditioner
— stuth leasachaidh
*— stu **lais**-ach-y*

— hair spray
— fras fuilt
*—fras **fulj***

Laundry

The dryer is too hot
Tha an tiormadair ro theth
*Ha uhn **jeer**-mad-er ro **hai***

The water is too hot
Tha an t-uisge ro theth
*Ha uhn **tush**-kyuh ro **hai***

Laundry

Is there a laundrette nearby?
Bheil taigh-nighe faisg air laimh?
***Vail** tie-**nee**-uh fashk air **liev**?*

How does the washing machine work?
Ciamar a tha an t-inneal-nighe ag obair?
***Cya**-mar uh ha uhn jeen-al-**nee**-uh ak **ohb**-ir?*

How long will it take?
De'n uine bheir e?
*Jayn **oon**-yuh vair e?*

Can you — clean this skirt?
An urrainn dhuibh — an sgiort seo ghlanadh?
   *Uhn **ur**-in yeev — uhn **skyuhrt** sho **ghlan**-ugh?*

     — clean and press these shirts
     — na leintean seo ghlanadh is iar-
      naigeadh?
     *— na **lay**-juhn sho **ghlan**-ugh iss **eer**-
      nik-ugh?*

191

Laundry

Can you wash these clothes?
An urrainn dhuibh na h-aodaichean seo nighe?
*Uhn **ur**-in yeev na **haod**-ich-an sho **nee**-uh?*

> **This stain is — oil**
> Se am ball seo — ola
> *Shem bowl sho — **ol**-uh*

> **— ink**
> **— dubh**
> *— du*

This fabric is delicate
Tha an t-aodach seo grinn
*ha uhn **taod**-ach sho **green***

I have lost my dry cleaning ticket
Tha mi air mo bhileag glanaidh a chall
*Ha mee air moh **veel**-ak **glan**-y uh chowl*

Please send it to this address
Cuir dhan t-seoladh seo e, le'r toil
*Cur dhan **jawl**-ugh sho e, lair tol*

When will I come back?
Cuin a thilleas mi?
*Cun uh **heel**-as mee?*

When will my clothes be ready?
Cuin a bhios m'aodach deiseil?
*Cun a vees **maod**-ach **jaish**-al?*

192

General repairs

I will come back — later
    Tillidh mi — nas anmoich
    Jeel-y mee — nas an-am-ich

          — in an hour
          — an ceann uair
          — uhn cyown oo-ar

General repairs

        This is — broken
        Tha seo — briste
        Ha sho — breesh-juh

          —damaged
          —air a mhilleadh
          —air uh veel-yugh

          — torn
          —sracte
          —strach-juh

Can you repair it?
An urrainn dhuibh a charadh?
Uhn ur-in yeev uh chaar-ugh?

Can you do it quickly?
An urrainn dhuibh a dheanamh sgiobalta?
Uhn ur-in yeev uh yen-iv skeep-alt-uh

At the post office

Have you got a spare part for this?
Bheil pairt agaibh son seo?
*Vail **paarsj** ak-iv son sho?*

Would you have a look at this please?
An seall sibh ri seo, le'r toil?
*Uhn **showl** sheev ree sho, lair tol*

Here is the guarantee
Seo am barrantas
*Sho uhm **bar**-ant-as*

At the post office

Most towns and large villages have a post office, normally open from 9.30am until 5pm on weekdays. Some of them may close for an hour at lunchtime and most are closed on Saturday afternoons. Postage stamps can be bought at newsagents, hotels and service stations.

12 stamps please
Dusan stamp, le'r toil
***Du**-san stamp, lair tol*

I need to send this by courier
Feumaidh mi seo a chur le teachdair
***Fay**-my mee sho uh chur lai **jech**-ker*

I want to send a telegram
Tha mi son teleagram a chur
*Ha mee son **tel**-ak-ram uh chur*

194

Using the telephone

I want to send this by registered mail
Tha mi son seo a chur le post claraichte
*Ha mee son sho uh chur lai post **claar-ich-juh***

I want to send this parcel
Tha mi son am parsail seo a chur
*Ha mee son uhm **par**-sel sho uh chur*

When will it arrive?
Cuin a ruigeas e?
*cun uh **rik**-as e*

How much is a letter to — **Spain?**
De chosgas litir do — an Spainn?
Jay** chos-kas **lee**-jir do* — *uhn **Spaan?

— **the United States?**
— na Staitean Aonaichte?
— *na **Staaj**-uhn **Aon**-ich-juh*

Can I have six stamps for postcards to France?
Faigh mi sia stampaichean son cairtean dhan Fhrain
*Fie mee **shee**-a **stamp**-ich-uhn son **cars**-juhn dhan **Rieng?***

Can I have a telegram form please?
Faigh mi bileag teleagram, le'r toil?
*Fie mee bee-lag **tel**—ak-ram, lair tol?*

Using the telephone

Standard phone numbers are made up of a five digit area code followed by a six digit number. If you are phoning

195

Using the telephone

locally within a specific area you need only use the latter six digits, though if you are phoning another area you need the area code. On a mobile phone you should use the whole number for local calls. Public phone boxes normally take 5p, 10p, 20p, 50p and £1 coins, or phone cards which can be purchased at service stations and other shops.

Can I use the telephone, please?
Faod mi am fon a chleachdadh, le'r toil?
*Faod mee uhm **foen** uh **chlech**-kuh, lair tol*

Can I dial direct?
An toir na putain direach troimhe mi?
*Uhn tawr na put-en **jeer**-ach tre-uh mee?*

Can you connect me with the international operator?
An cuir sibh dhan t-seirbhis eadarnaiseanta mi?
*Uhn cur sheev dhan **jair**-av-ish ait-er-**naash**-ant-uh mee?*

Have you got any change?
Bheil iomlaid agaibh?
*Vail **yum-lej ak**-iv?*

How do I use the telephone?
Ciamar a chleachdas mi am fon?
*Cya-mar uh **chlech**-kas mee uhm **foen**?*

How much is it to phone to London?
De tha e fonadh gu Lunnainn?
*Jay ha e **foen**-ugh gu **Lun**-in?*

Using the telephone

I must make a phone call to France
Feumaidh mi fonadh dhan Fhraing
*Fay-my mee foen-ugh dhan **Rieng***

I need to make a phone call
Feumaidh mi fonadh
Fay-my mee foen-ugh

What is the code for Spain?
De an aireamh son an Spainn?
*Jayn **aar-iv** son uhn Spaan?*

I would like to make a reversed charge call
Bu mhath leam fonadh le paigheadh thall
*Bu va lum foen-ugh le **paa-yuh** howl*

The number I need is . . .
Se an aireamh tha dhith orm . . .
*She uhn **aar-iv** ha yee or-am . . .*

What is the charge?
De a' chosgais?
*Jay uh **chos**-kish?*

Please call me back
Fon air ais, le'r toil
Foen air ash, lair tol

I am sorry, We were cut off
Tha mi duilich. Chaidh ar gearradh dhe
*Ha mee **dil**-ich. **Chie** ar **gyar**-ugh ye*

Using the telephone

The number is out of order
Chan eil an aireamh ag obair
*Chan ail uhn **aar**-iv ak **ohb**-ir*

The number is engaged
Tha an aireamh trang
*Ha uhn **aar**-iv **trang***

I am trying to get through
Tha mi fiachainn ri faighinn troimhe
*Ha mee **fee**-ach-in ree **fie**-in tre-uh*

Please go ahead
Toisichibh, le'r toil
***Taw**-shich-iv, lair tol*

Hello, is that the manager?
Hullo, an e sin am manaidsear?
*Huhl-o, uhn e sheen uhm **man**-ij-er?*

I want to speak to Mr Campbell
Tha mi son bruidheann ri Maighstir Caimbeul
*Ha mee son **bru**-yin ree **Miesh**-jir **Ciem**-bal*

I cannot obtain the number
Chan urrainn dhomh an aireamh fhaighinn
*Chan **ur**-in dho uhn **aar**-iv **ie**-in*

Changing money

Changing money

Can I contact my bank to arrange a transfer?
Faod mi bruidheann ri mo bhanca son airgiod a chur anall
*Faod mee **bru-yin** ree moh **vank-uh** son **er**-ak-ad uh chur a-nowl*

Has my cash arrived?
An d'rainig m'airgiod?
*Uhn **draan**-ik **mer**-ak-ad?*

I would like a cash advance with my credit card
Bu thoigh leam airgiod air thoiseach le mo chairt creideis
*Bu hie lum **er**-ak-ad air **hosh**-ach lai moh **charsj craij**-ish*

This is the name and address of my bank
Seo ainm is seoladh mo bhanca
*Sho **en**-im iss **shaw**-lugh moh **vank**-uh*

Can I change	**— these travellers' cheques?**
Faigh mi airgiod air	— na seicean siubhail seo?
*Fie mee **er**-ak-ad air*	*—— na **shaik**-uhn **shu**-il sho?*

	— these notes?
	— na notaichean seo?
	*— na **not**-ich-uhn sho?*

Here is my passport
Seo mo chead-siubhail
*Sho moh chyait-**shu**-il*

199

Changing money

What is the rate of exchange?
De an luach malairt a th'ann?
*Jay uhn **loo**-ach **mal**-erj uh hown?*

What is the rate for — sterling?
De an luach a th'air — puinnd Shasannach?
*Jayn **loo**-ach uh hair — punj **Has**-an-ach?*

— dollars?
— dolairean?
*— **dol**-er-uhn*

What is you commission?
De do chuibhrionn?
*Jay do **chuy**-ron?*

HEALTH

During normal shopping hours drugs and advice are available from the nearest chemist's shops. At other times service stations and supermarkets carry a basic range of medicines such as pain-killers and cough mixtures. For more serious ailments the local police, or some other local source, should be able to advise where the nearest doctor or medical facilities can be found. All hospitals in the area can provide basic accidennt and emergency services, though they might be at some distance since hospital facilities within the Highlands are organised on an area basis.

What's wrong?

I need a doctor
Tha feum agam air dotair
*Ha **faym ak**-am air **dot**-er*

Can I see a doctor?
Faic mi dotair?
Fiec mee dot-er?

He is hurt
Tha e leointe
*Ha e **lyawn**-juh*

What's wrong

She has been badly injured
Chaidh a droch ghortachadh
*Chie uh droch **ghors**-dach-ugh*

He has burnt himself
Loisg e e fhein
***Lushk** e e hayn*

He has dislocated his shoulder
Chaidh e amach air a ghualainn
*Chie e am-**ach** air uh **ghoo**-al-in*

He is unconscious
Tha e gun chainnt
*Ha e gun **chienj***

He has a temperature
Tha e fiabhrasach
*Ha e **fee**-ar-as-ach*

She has been bitten
Chaidh a bideadh
*Chie uh **bee**-jugh*

My son has cut himself
Ghearr mo mhac e fhein
***Yaar** moh **vachk** e hayn*

My son is ill
Tha mo mhac tinn
*Ha moh **vachk jeen***

202

What's wrong

I am ill
Tha mi tinn
Ha mee jeen

I am a diabetic
Tha ruith-fhual orm
Ha ruy-oo-al or-am

I am allergic to penicillin
Tha penisilion a' dol gu droch ire dhomh
Ha pen-is-il-in uh dol gu droch eer-uh gho

I am badly sunburnt
Tha droch losgadh grein orm
Ha droch luhs-kugh grayn or-am

I am constipated
Tha teannachadh orm
Ha jan-ach-ugh or-am

I cannot sleep
Chan urrainn dhomh cadal
Chan ur-in gho cad-al

I feel dizzy
Tha tuaineal orm
Ha too-an-yal or-am

I feel faint
Tha laigse orm
Ha lieksh or-am

What's wrong

I feel nauseous
Tha sannt diobhairt oram
Ha sownt jeev-erj or-am

I fell
Thuit mi
Huj mee

I have a pain here
Tha cradh an seo
Ha craagh uhn sho

I have a rash here
Tha broth an seo
Ha bro uhn sho

I have been sick
Bha mi diobhairt
Va mee jeev-erj

I have been stung
Chaidh mo lot
Chie moh lot

I have cut myself
Ghearr mi mi fhein
Yaar mee mee hayn

I have diarrhoea
Tha sput orm
Ha spoot or-am

204

What's wrong

I have pulled a muscle
Tharraing mi feidh
Har-ing mee fay

I have sunstroke
Bhuail buille-greine mi
Voo-al bul-yuh-gray-nuh mee

I suffer from high blood pressure
Tha mi a' fulang bruthadh fala
Ha mee uh ful-ag broo-ugh fal-a

I think I have food poisoning
Cha chreid mi nach eil truailleadh-bidh orm
Cha chraij mee nach ail troo-il-yugh-bee or-am

It is inflamed here
Tha e air at an seo
Ha e air at uhn sho

My arm is broken
Tha mo ghairdean briste
Ha moh ghaar-jan breesh-juh

My stomach is upset
Tha mo stamag troimh cheile
Ha moh stam-ag tre chyay-luh

My tongue is coated
Tha li air mo theanga
Ha lee air moh heng-uh

205

What's wrong

There is a swelling here
Tha at an seo
*Ha **at** uhn sho*

    I have hurt — my arm
    Ghortaich mi — mo ghairdean
    *Ghawrs-jich mee — moh **ghaar**-jan*

        — my leg
        — mo chas
        *— moh **chas***

    It is painful — to walk
    Tha e craiteach — coiseachd
    *Ha e **craaj**-ach — **cosh**-achk*

        — to breathe
        — anail a tharraing
        *— **an**-el uh **har**-ing*

        — to swallow
        — slugadh
        *— **sluk**-ugh*

    I have — a headache
    Tha — ceann goirt agam
    *Ha — cyown **gorshj** ak-am*

        —a sore throat
        —amhach ghoirt agam
        *—**av**-ach **ghorshj** ak-am*

What's wrong

I have — an earache
Tha —greim cluaise orm
*Ha —graim **cloo**-ish-uh or-am*

I am taking these drugs
Tha mi gabhail na drugaichean seo
*Ha mee **gav**-el na **druhk**-ich-uhn sho*

Can you give me a prescription for them?
An toir sibh dhomh bileag air an son?
*Uhn **tawr** sheev gho **beel**-ak air uhn son*

I am on the pill
Tha mi gabhail a' phile
*Ha mee **gav**-el uh **feel**-uh*

I am pregnant
Tha mi trom
*Ha mee **trowm***

My blood group is . . .
Se gne m'fhala . . .
*She gre **mal**-uh . . .*

I do not know my blood group
Chan aithne dhomh gne m'fhala
*Chan **an**-yuh gho gre **mal**-uh*

I need some antibiotics
Feumaidh mi antibiotaic
***Fay**-my mee **ant**-y-bee-ot-ec*

207

At the hospital

Do I have to go into hospital?
Feum mi dhol astigh dhan ospadal?
Faym mee ghol as-tie ghan osp-ad-al?

Do I need an operation?
Feum mi dhol fo lannsa?
Faym mee ghol foh lown-sa

At the hospital

Here is my E-111 form
Seo mo bhileag E-111 (ceud is aon-deug)
Sho moh veel-ak E-111 (cee-ad is aon-jee-ak)

How do I get reimbursed?
Ciamar a gheibh mi airgiod air ais?
Cya-mar uh yaiv mee er-ik-ad air ash

Must I stay in bed?
Feum mi fuireach 'sa leabaidh?
Fayn mee fur-ach suh lep-y

When will I be able to travel?
Cuin a theid agam air siubhal?
Cun uh haid ak-am air shoo-il

Will I be able to go out tomorrow?
Am bi mi air chomas dhol amach am maireach?
Uhm bee mee air choh-mas ghol a-mach am maar-ach?

208

Parts of the body

ankle
aobrann
ao-brin

ear
cluas
cloo-*as*

arm
gairdean
gaar-jan

elbow
uileann
ul-*uhn*

back
druim
dreem

eye
suil
sool

bone
cnamh
craav

face
aodann
aod-*uhn*

breast
broilleach
brol-*yach*

finger
corrag
cor-*ag*

cheek
gruaidh
groo-*iy*

foot
cas
cas

chest
cliabh
clee-*av*

hand
lamh
laav

209

Parts of the body

heart
cridhe
cree-uh

kidney
airne
aar-nyuh

knee
glun
gloon

leg
cas
cas

liver
gruthan
groo-an

lungs
sgamhan
sgav-an

mouth
beul
bee-al

muscle
feith
fay

neck
amhach
av-ach

nose
sron
strawn

skin
craiceann
criek-in

stomach
stamag
stam-ag

throat
sgornan
skawrn-an

wrist
caol-duirn
caol-doorn

At the dentist's

I have to see the dentist
Feumaidh mi am fiaclair fhaicinn
*Fay-my mee uhm fee-ach-cler **iech**-kin*

I have a toothache
Tha an deideadh orm
*Ha uhn **jay**-juh or-am*

Are you going to fill it?
Bheil sibh dol 'ga lionadh?
*Vail sheev dol ga **lee**-uhn-ugh?*

I have broken a tooth
Tha mi air fiacal a bhristeadh
*Ha mee air **fee**-ach-cal uh **vreesh**-juh*

Will you have to take it out?
Feum sibh a tharraing?
*Faym sheev uh **har**-ing?*

My false teeth are broken
Tha m'fhiaclan fuadain briste
*Ha **mee**-ach-clan **foo**-ad-en **breesh**-juh*

Can you repair them?
An urrainn dhuibh an caradh?
*Uhn **ur**-in yeev uhn **caar**-ugh*

211

At the dentist's

My gums are sore
Tha mo chairean goirt
*Ha moh **chaar**-uhn **gorshj***

Please give me an injection
Thoir steall dhomh, le'r toil
*Hawr **shtyowl** gho, lair tol*

That hurts
Tha sin goirt
*Ha sheen **gorshj***

The filling has come out
Tha an lionadh air tighinn as
*Ha uhn **lee-uhn**-ugh air **jeen** as*

This one hurts
Tha am fear seo goirt
*Ha uhm fer sho **gorshj***

FOR YOUR INFORMATION

Numbers

1
aon
aon

2
da/dha
da/dha

3
tri
tree

4
ceithir
cyai-hir

5
coig
coh-ik

6
sia
shee-a

7
seachd
shechk

8
ochd
ochk

9
naoi
nao

10
deich
jaich

11
aon-deug
aon-jee-ak

12
dha-dheug
ghaa-ghee-ak

13
tri-deug
tree-jee-ak

14
ceithir-deug
cyai-hir-jee-ak

15
coig-deug
coh-ik-jee-ak

16
sia-deug
shee-a-jee-ak

17
seachd-deug
shechk-jee-ak

18
ochd-deug
ochk-jee-ak

Numbers

19
naoi–deug
nao-jee-ak

20
fichead
feech-ad

21
fichead is aon
feech-ad is aon

22
fichead is dha
feech-ad is ghaa

23
fichead is tri
feech-ad is tree

24
fichead is ceithir
feech-ad is cyai-hir

25
fichead is coig
feech-ad is coh-ik

26
fichead is sia
feech-ad is shee-a

27
fichead is seachd
feech-ad is shechk

28
fichead is ochd
feech-ad is ochk

29
fichead is naoi
feech-ad is nao

30
trithead
tree-ad

40
ceathrad
cyer-ad

50
leth–cheud
lai-chee-ad

60
seasgad
shaisk-ad

70
seachdad
shechk-ad

80
ochdad
ochd-ad

90
naochad
naoch-ad

100
ceud
cyee-ad

200
da cheud
daa chee-ad

300
tri cheud
tree chee-ad

400
ceithir cheud
cyai-hir chee-ad

500
coig ceud
coh-ik cyee-ad

600
sia ceud
shee-a cyee-ad

Ordinal numbers

700
seachd ceud
shechk cyee-ad

1000
mile
meel-uh

4000
ceithir mile
cyai-hir meel-uh

800
ochd ceud
ochk cyee-ad

2000
da mhile
daa veel-uh

1000000
millean
meel-yan

900
naoi ceud
nao cyee-ad

3000
tri mile
tree meel-uh

Ordinal numbers

1st
a' cheud
a' chyee-ad

4th
an ceathramh
uhn cyer-iv

2nd
an darna
uhn darn-uh

5th
an coigeamh
uhn coh-ik-iv

3rd
an treas
uhn trais

nth
an eneamh
uhn en-iv

Fractions and percentages

Fractions and percentages

a half
leth
lyai

a quarter
cairteal
cars-jal

a third
trian
tree-an

two thirds
da thrian
daa hree-an

10 per cent
deich 'sa cheud
jaich suh chyee-ad

Days

Sunday
Didomhnaich
Jee-dawn-ich

Monday
Diluain
Jee-loo-en

Tuesday
Dimairt
Jee-maarsj

Wednesday
Diciadain
Jee-cyee-ad-in

Thursday
Diardaoin
Jee-ard-aon

Friday
Dihaoine
Jee-haon-yuh

Saturday
Disatharna
Jee-sa-har-nuh

The seasons

Dates

on Friday
Dihaoine
*Jee-**haon**-yuh*

next Tuesday
Dimairt-sa tighinn
*Jee-**maarsj**-suh jeen*

last Tuesday
Dimairt-sa chaidh
*Jee-**maarsj**-suh **chie**-y*

yesterday
an de
uhn jay

today
an diugh
uhn ju

tomorrow
am maireach
*uhm **maar**-ach*

in June
'san Ogmhios
*san **Awk**-vees*

July 7th
an seachdamh dhen Iuchair
*an **shechk**-iv yen **Yuch**-ir*

next week
an ath sheachdain
*uhn **a hechk**-in*

last month
a' mhios-sa chaidh
*uh **vees**-suh **chie**-y*

The seasons

spring
an t-earrach
*uhn **jar**-ach*

summer
an samhradh
*uhn **sow**-rugh*

autumn
am foghar *uhm*
***foh**-ar*

winter
an geamhradh
*uhn **gyow**-rugh*

217

Times of the year

Times of the year

in spring
as t-earrach
*as **jar**-ach*

in summer
as t-samhradh
*as **tow**-rugh*

in autumn
as t-fhoghar
*as **toh**-ar*

in winter
'sa gheamhradh
*suh **yow**-rugh*

Months

January
am Faoilleach
*uhm **Faol**-yach*

February
an Gearran
*uhn **Gyar**-an*

March
am Mairt
*uhm **Maarsj***

April
an Giblean
*uhn **Geep**-lan*

May
am Maigh
*uhm **Maa**-y*

June
an t-Ogmhios
*uhn **Tawk**-vees*

July
an t-Iuchair
*uhn **Tyuch**-er*

August
an Linasdal
*uhn **Loon**-as-dal*

September
an t-Sultainn
*uhn **Tul**-tin*

October
an Damhair
*uhn **Dav**-ir*

218

Colours

November
an t-Samhainn
*uhn **Tav**-in*

December
an Dubhlachd
*uhn **Dool**-achk*

Special days

January 1, New Year's Day
La na Bliadhna Uire
*La na Bleen **Oor**-uh*

January 25, Burns Night
Oidhche Bhurns
Iech**-uh **Vuhrns

Easter Sunday
Didomhnaich Caisge
***Jee-dawn**-ich **Caashk**-yuh*

October 31, Hallowe'en
Oidhche Shamhna
***Iech**-uh **How**-nuh*

November 30, St Andrew's Day
La Naomh Anndrais
*La Naov **Own**-drish*

December 25, Christmas Day
La na Nollaig
*La na **Nolb**-ek*

Colours

black
dubh
du

blue
gorm
***gor**-am*

brown
donn
down

rust
ruadh
***roo**-ugh*

219

Common adjectives

fawn
lachdann
lach-kuhn

purple
purpaidh
pur-py

gold
or
awr

red
dearg
jer-ak

green
uaine
oo-an-yuh

silver
airgiod
er-ik-ad

grey
glas
glas

tan
odhar
oh-ar

orange
orains
or-inj

white
geal
gyal

pink
pionc
pink

yellow
buidhe
buy-uh

Common adjectives

angry
feargach
fer-ak-ach

bad
dona
don-uh

Common adjectives

beautiful
alainn
aal-in

big
mor
moer

bright
soilleir
suhl-ir

broad
leathann
lai-han

cheap
saor
saor

cold
fuar
foo-ar

dark
dorcha
dor-ach-a

difficult
doirbh
dair-iv

dry
tioram
jeer-am

easy
soirbh
sair-iv

fast
luath
loo-a

fat
reamhar
raa-uhr

fierce
borb
bor-ib

gentle
socair
sok-ir

good
math
ma

hard
cruaidh
croo-y

221

Common adjectives

high
ard
aard

hot
teth
tyai

little
beag
baik

long
fada
fat-uh

narrow
tana
tan-uh

new
ur
oor

old
sean
shen

peaceful
sitheil
shee-hil

short
goirid
guhr-ij

slow
mall
mowl

small
biodach
beed-ach

soft
bog
bohk

thin
caol
caol

ugly
grannda
graad-uh

wet
fliuch
fluch

Signs and notices

allowed only for . . .
ceadaichte amhain son . . .
cyaid-ich-juh uh-vaan son..

ambulance
carbad-eiridinn
car-ab-ad-air-ij-in

arrivals
air tighinn
air jeen

bank
banca
banc-uh

beware of the dog
an aire dhan chu
uhn ar-uh ghan choo

cashier
ionmhasair
yun-av-as-er

caution
an aire
uhn ar-uh

charge
astaigh gun chosgais
uh-stie gun chosk-ish

closed
duinte
doon-juh

closed in the afternoon
duinte feasgar
doon-juh fais-gar

closing down sale
feill dhunaidh
fayl ghoon-y

communication cord
ball rabhaidh
bowl roh-y

cold
fuar
foo-ar

Customs
Cuspainn
Cus-pin

223

Signs and notices

cycle path
ceum baidhsagal
*cyaim **bie**-sak-al*

danger
cunnart
cun-art

danger of death
cunnart beatha
cun-art be-huh

danger of fire
cunnart teine
cun-art jeen-uh

departures
fagail
faak-el

diversion
cuairt
coo-arsj

do not lean out
na crom amach
*na crowm uh-**mach***

do not touch
na buin
*na **bun***

drinking water
uisge ol
*ishk **awl***

emergency exit
amach an eiginn
*uh-**mach** uhn ayk-in*

employees only
luchd-obrach amhain
*luchk-**ohb**-rach uh-**vaan***

enter without knocking
astaigh gun ghnogadh
*uh-**stie** gun **ghrok**-ugh*

entrance
astaigh
*uh-**stie***

exit
amach
*uh-**mach***

for external use only
cleachd amuigh amhain
*clechk uh-**muy** uh-**vaan***

for sale
ri reic
*ree **raichk***

224

Signs and notices

fire alarm
rabhadh teine
roh-ugh jain-uh

fire brigade
luchd smalaidh
luchk-smaal-y

gentlemen
fir
feer

hospital
ospadal
osp-ad-al

information
fiosrachadh
fees-rach-ugh

keep off the grass
cum far an fheoir
coom far uhn yawr

keep to the right
cum gu deas
coom gu jais

ladies
mnathan
mraa-uhn

lift
ardaichear
aard-ich-er

litter
smodal
smod-al

lost property office
oifis cuid chaillte
of-ish cuj chiel-juh

no entry
na teid astaigh
na jaid uh-stie

no picture taking
na tog dealbh
na tohk jal-iv

no thoroughfare
slighe dhuinte
shlee-uh ghoon-juh

no smoking
na smoc
na smochk

225

Signs and notices

no talking to driver when moving
na bruidhinn ris an draibhear 's e gluasad
na breen reesh uhn drie-ver se gloo-as-ad

no trespassing
cum na criochan
coom na cree-ach-in

occupied
an sas
uhn saas

open
fosgailte
fosk-il-juh

parking for residents
pairceadh luchd-comhnaidh
paark-yuh luchk-cawn-y

poison
puinnsean
puy-shen

police
polais
pol-ish

price list
clar-pris
claar-preesh

private road
rathad priobhaideach
raad preev-ej-ach

pull
tarraing
taring

push
put
put

reserved
gleidhte
glay-juh

ring
seinn
shien

sale
feill
fayl

school
sgoil
sgol

226

Signs and notices

smoking area
aite smocaidh
aaj-uh smok-y

smoking compartment
seomar smocaidh
shaw-mar smoch-ky

sold out
buileach reicte
bul-ach raichk-juh

special offer
tairgse araid
tair-iksh aar-ij

souvenirs
cuimhneachain
cuy-nach-en

telephone
fon
foen

to let
ri fhasdadh
ree asd-ugh

travel agency
ionad siubhail
een-ad shoo-il

timetable
clar-ama
claar-am-uh

vacant
falamh
fal-iv

welcome
failte
faal-juh

IN AN EMERGENCY

What to do

In all types of emergencies the police are the first port of call. Such incidents as theft or the loss of a wallet with personal cards should be reported immediately to the nearest police station. In major emergencies – such as serious road accidents, outbreaks of fire that cannot be controlled, or life-threatening accidents in the hill or at sea – the emergency services should be alerted by phoning the three digit emergency numbers 999 or 112. Fullest details should be given, especially location, and some estimate as to what services are required – police, medical and ambulance, or fire brigade, or indeed all three.

Call — the fire brigade
Gairm air — an luchd-smalaidh
*Guhr-am air — uhn **luchk-smal**-y*

— the police
— a' pholais
*— uh **fol**-ish*

What to do

Call — an ambulance
Gairm air — carbad eiridinn
Guhr-am air — car-ab-ad air-ij-in

Get a doctor
Faigh dotair
Fie dot-er

There is a fire
Tha teine ann
Ha jeen-uh own

Where is — the hospital?
Caite bheil — an t-ospadal?
Caa-juh vail — uhn tosp-ad-al

— the police station?
— steisean nam polas?
— stay-shen nam pol-as

PLACE NAMES

Place names can tell you a lot about the territory you are passing through if only you can unravel the key to their meaning. Many Scottish names, and most Highland names, are really Gaelic names disguised under a thin veneer of Anglicised spelling. The clerks and civil servants who first wrote them down were largely based in Edinburgh, the centre of Scottish government before union with the English parliament in 1707, and few of them had any knowledge of Gaelic. They had to try to transcribe the Gaelic sounds they heard from the lips of the local people to paper using their conventional English orthography. Thus **Inverness**, the capital of the Highlands, is an Anglicised approximation for the original Gaelic *Inbhirnis,* meaning "the mouth of the river Ness". Similarly, **Kingussie** is a none-too-successful attempt to convey the sound of its Gaelic name *Ceann-a-ghiuthsaich*, which means "the head of the pine wood": and *Tobair-mhoire* in Mull, which means "Mary's well", emerges as **Tobermory**. Most of the Highland place names you see on modern road maps are a product of this process.

In other cases the bureaucrats overcame their problem by ignoring the Gaelic sound of a name and simply translating its meaning directly into English. **Broadford** in Skye bears

Towns

no relationship to the sound of its original Gaelic name *An t-Ath-leathann,* but it does translate its exact meaning into English quite succinctly. **Newtonmore**, "the new town on the moor", does the same for *Bail-ur an t-Sleibh,* though the English and Gaelic versions sound very different.

And in yet a third, though small, category of place names the English and Gaelic versions have absolutely no relationship to each other, either in sound or meaning. Two well-known Highland towns, **Fort William** and **Fort Augustus**, are prime examples. Their names reflect 17th- and 18th-century history, when the Hanoverian forces finally subdued a Gaelic populace with largely Jacobite sympathies. The Gaels refused to adopt the names by giving them Gaelic versions. They called **Fort William** *An Gearasdan,* "the garrison", grudgingly admitting its dominating influence, and they still refer to **Fort Augustus** by its old name of *Cille-chuimein,* "St Colman's church".

And just to add a little bit more colour to the broth of Highland place names, some of the names that follow contain Norse elements, reflecting the pre-10th century era when the Vikings raided and settled in many of the Western Isles and much of the west coast of Scotland – a time before Gaelic became the dominant language in the area.

Aberdeen
Abaireadhain
Ap-er-ay-en
Mouth of river Don

Aberfeldy
Abair-pheallaidh
Ap-er-fyal-y
Mouth of river Paldoc

Towns

Acharacle
Ath-tharcaill
*A-**har**-a-gil*
Torquil's ford (personal name)

Applecross
A' Chomraich
*Uh-**chohm**-rich*
The sanctuary

Ardrishaig
Airdriseig
*Aard-**reesh**-ek*
Headland of the thorny bay

Armadale
Armadal
*Ar-**am**-ad-al*
Arm-shaped valley

Aultbea
An t-Allt-beithe
*Uhn-towlt-**bai**-uh*
Stream of the birch trees

Aviemore
An Aghaidh-mhor
*Uhn-agh-y-**voer***
The big rock face

Balivanich
Baile-mhanaich
*Bal-uh-**van**-ich*
Town of the monks

Ballachulish
Baile-chaolais
*Bal-uh-**chaol**-ish*
Town of the narrows

Ballinluig
Bail-an-luig
*Bal-an-**lik***
Township in the hollow

Bettyhill
Am Blaran Odhar
*Uhm-**blaar**-an-**oh**-ar*
The small grey field

Blair Atholl
Blar-athall
*Blaar-**a**-hal*
Plain of new Ireland

Boat of Garten
Coite Ghartain
*Co-juh-**ghars**-jen*
Ferry of the river Garten

232

Bowmore
Am Bogha-mor
Uhm-boh-moer
The big hut

Broadford
An t-Ath-leathann
Uhn-taa-lai-han
The broad ford

Brora
Bruraidh
Broo-rie
River of the bridge

Campbeltown
Ceannloch-chille-chiarain
Cyan-loch-cheel-yuh-cheer-en
Head of St Kieran's loch

Carrbridge
Drochaid Charra
Droch-ij-char-uh
Bridge of the rock shelf

Castlebay
Bagh a' Chaisteil
Baagh-uh-chash-jel
Bay of the castle

Craignure
Creag-an-iubhair
Craik-uhn-yew-er
Yew tree rock

Crianlaraich
A' Chrian-laraich
Uh-chree-an-lar-ich
The little pass

Crieff
Craoibh
Cru-eev
Place of trees

Dalwhinnie
Dail-chuinnidh
Dal-choon-y
Field of the champion

Dingwall
Inbhir-pheofharain
Een-er-fyo-ar-en
Mouth of river Peffery

Dornoch
Dornach
Dawr-nach
Place of pebbles

233

Towns

Drumnadrochit
Druim-na-drochaid
*Dreem-na-**droch**-ij*
Ridge of the bridge

Dunblane
Dun-blathain
*Dun-**blaa**-en*
Fort of St Blane

Dundee
Dun-de
*Dun-**jay***
Fort of Daig (personal name)

Dunkeld
Dun-chaillinn
*Dun-**chal**-ing*
Fort of the Caledonians

unvegan
Dun-bheagain
*Dun-**vaik**-en*
Beagan's fort (personal name)

Durness
Diur-nis
__Joor__-neesh
Headland of deer

Edinburgh
Dun-eideann
*Dun-**ay**-juhn*
Fort of the rock face

Fionnphort
Fionnaphort
__Fyun__-uh-forst
White harbour

Fort Augustus
Cille-chuimein
*Keel-uh-**cheem**-en*
St Colman's church

Fort William
An Gearasdan
*Uhn **Ger**-as-tan*
The garrison

Gairloch
Gearrloch
__Gyaar__-loch
The short loch

Glasgow
Glaschu
__Glas__-cho
The green place

234

Towns

Golspie
Goillspidh
Giel-shpee
Gulli's farm (personal name)

Inveraray
Inbhir-aora
Een-er-aor-a
Mouth of smooth river

Invergarry
Inbhir-garaidh
Een-er-gar-y
Mouth of the rough river

Inverness
Inbhirnis
Een-er-neesh
Mouth of river Ness

Kingussie
Ceann-ghiuthsaich
Cyan-yoos-ich
Head of the pine wood

Kinlochbervie
Ceannloch-beirbhidh
Cyan-loch-bair-uh-vy
Head of the stormy loch

Kyle of Lochalsh
Caol Loch-aillse
Caol-loch-iesh-uh
Narrows of the spectre loch

Kyleakin
Caol-acainn
Caol-aach-kin
The narrows of Haakon (Norse king)

Leverburgh
An t-Ob
Uhn-tawp
The bay

Lochaline
Loch-alainn
Loch-aal-in
The beautiful loch

Lochboisdale
Loch-baghasdal
Loch-bagh-as-dal
Loch of the dale bay

Lochgilphead
Ceannloch-gilb
Cyan-loch-geel-ib
Head of the chisel-shaped loch

235

Towns

Lochinver
Loch-an-inbhir
Loch-an-een-uh-ver
Loch of the river mouth

Lochmaddy
Loch-nam-madadh
Loch-nam-mat-ugh
Loch of the dogs

Mallaig
Malaig
Mal-ek
Headland bay

Newtonmore
Bail-ur an t-Sleibh
Bal-oor-uhn-tlayv
New town on the moor

Oban
An t-Oban
Uhn-tawp-an
The small bay

Perth
Peairt
Pyarst
Place of the bush

Pitlochry
Baile-chloichridh
Bal-uh-chloch-ree
Township of stones

Poolewe
Poll-iubh
Pohl-yew
Pool of the yew trees

Port Ellen
Port Eilidh
Porst-ail-y
Ellenor's harbour (personal name)

Portree
Portruigh
Porst-reegh
Harbour of the slope

Spean Bridge
Drochaid Spiothain
Droch-ij-spee-en
Bridge of river Spean

Stirling
Sruighle
Stree-lie
Field by the stream

Islands

Stornoway
Steornabhagh
Shtawr-na-vie
Steering bay

Tain
Baile-dhubhthaich
Bal-uh-ghu-hich
St Duthac's town

Tarbert
An Tairbeart
Uhn-tair-uh-berj
The isthmus

Taynuilt
Taigh-an-uillt
Tie-uhn-oo-ilj
House of the stream

Thurso
Inbhir-theorsa
Een-er-hyawr-suh
Mouth of bull river

Tobermory
Tobair-mhoire
Toh-per-vor-uh
Mary's well

Tomatin
Tom-aiteann
Towm-aj-uhn
The juniper hillock

Tyndrum
Taigh-an-droma
Tie-uhn-drum-uh
House of the ridge

Uig
Uige
Oog-yuh
The bay

Wick
Inbhir-uige
Een-er-oog-yuh
Mouth of bay river

Islands

Arran
Arainn
Ar-in
Peaked isle

Barra
Barraigh
Bar-ie
St Barr's island

237

Islands

Benbecula
Beinn-na-faoghla
Bien-uh-vao-luh
Hill of the fords

Bernaray
Bearnaraigh na Hearadh
Byarn-ar-ie-na-her-ugh
Bjorn's isle off Harris

Bute
Eilean Bhoid
Ail-an-vawj
Patch of land

Canna
Canaidh
Can-ie
Bucket shaped isle

Coll
Cola
Col-uh
Barren place

Eigg
Eige
Aik-uh
Notched isle

Eriskay
Eirisgeidh
Ayr- ish-kie
Erik's isle (personal name)

Fladda
Fladaigh
Flat-ie
Flat isle

Gigha
Giogha
Gyigh-ie
God's isle

Great Bernera
Bearnaraigh Leodhais
Byarn-ar-ie-loe-ish
Bjorn's isle (personal name)
off Lewis

Harris
Na Hearadh
Na-her-ugh
Higher island

Iona
I Chaluim-chille (usually I)
Ee-chal-im-cheel-yuh
(usually *Ee*)
St Columba's isle

238

Islands

Islay
Ile
Eel-uh
Ile's isle (personal name)

Jura
Diura
Joor-ie
Doirad's isle (personal name)

Kerrera
Cearara
Kyer-er-ie
Copse island

Lewis
Leodhas
Lyoe-as
People's home

Lismore
Liosmor
Lees-moer
Big garden

Luing
Luing
Loo-ing
Ship isle

Muck
Eilean nam Muc
Ail-an-na-muchk
Pig island

Mull
Muile
Mool-uh
Isle of headlands

North Uist
Uibhist-a-tuath
Ooy-isht-uh-too-a
North abode

Pabay
Pabaigh
Pab-ie
Priest isle

Raasay
Ratharsair
Raar-ser
Ridged isle of deer

Rum
Ruim
Rooym
Spacious isle

Islands

Scalpay
Scalpaigh
Scalp-ie
Ship isle

Scarba
Scarbaigh
Scar-ab-ie
Cormorant isle

Scarp
An Scarp
Uhn-scarp
The cliff isle

Seil
Saoil
Siel
Seal isle

Skye
An t-Eilean Sgitheanach
Uhn-jail-an-skee-han-ach
Winged isle

Soay
Soaidh
Saw-ie
Sheep isle

South Uist
Uibhist-a-deas
Ooy-isht-uh-jais
South abode

Staffa
Stafaidh
Staf-ie
Isle of pillars

Taransay
Tarasaigh
Tar-as-ie
St Taran's isle

Tiree
Tiriodh
Tyir-ugh
Land of corn

Ulva
Ulbha
Ool-uh-va
Wolf isle

Vatersay
Bhatarsaigh
Vat-er-sie
Glove isle